FACTS AT YOUR FINGERTIPS

GREAT SCIENTISTS
PHYSICAL SCIENCES

BROWN
BEAR
BOOKS

Published by Brown Bear Books Limited

An imprint of:
The Brown Reference Group Ltd
68 Topstone Road
Redding
Connecticut 06896
USA

www.brownreference.com

Library of Congress Cataloging-in-Publication Data
available upon request

ISBN-13 978-1-933834-46-7

Editorial Director: Lindsey Lowe
Managing Editor: Tim Harris
Project Director: Graham Bateman
Designer: Steve McCurdy
Editor: Derek Hall

Printed in the United States of America

Picture Credits

Abbreviations: AKG Archiv für Kunst und Geschichte,
London; BAL Bridgeman Art Library; C Corbis; MEPL Mary
Evans Picture Library; SPL Science Photo Library; b=bottom;
c=center; t=top; l=left; r=right.

Cover Images
Front: *Albert Einstein,* Library of Congress
Back: *Marie Curie,* Jupiter/Photos.com

1, 3 Photos.com; 4 By courtesy of the National Portrait
Gallery, London; 5t The Royal Institution, London/BAL; 5b
Lincolnshire County Council, Usher Gallery, Lincoln/BAL; 6-
7 Alfred Pasieka/SPL; 7r ARPL; 8-9 Bettmann/C; 9 Private
Collection; 12 Philip de Bay/C; 13 Michael Holford/Royal
Institution, London; 14t Philadelphia Museum of Art/C;
14b Bettmann/C; 15t Hulton-Deutsch Collection/C; 15b
ARPL; 16-17 C; 17 Royal Institution, London; 20
Underwood & Underwood/C; 21 MEPL; 22 SPL; 22-23, 23t
Jean-Loup Charmet/SPL; 23b Museum of the History of
Science, Oxford; 24t Bettmann/C; 24c C; 25 Bettmann/C;
26t ARPL; 26c Bodleian Library, Oxford; 26b Cavendish
Laboratory/University of Cambridge; 27 Curie Institute
Archives; 30 Bettmann/C; 31 Institute International de
Physique Solvay/AIP Niels Bohr Library; 32 AKG Berlin; 34
Illustrated London News Picture Library; 36tl Brown
Reference Group; 36tr Private Collection; 36b From
"Quantum Universe"; 37t Austrian Archives/C; 37b C; 40l
MEPL; 40r Hulton/Archive; 41 Bettmann/C; 42-43 Roger
Ressmeyer/C; 43t MEPL; 43b C; 45t Kevin R. Morris/C;
45b, 46 Science Museum/SSPL; 48 Science Museum/SSPL;
49 Bettmann/C; 50, 51t C; 51b Chicago Historical Society;
52l Hulton-Deutsch Collection/C; 52r Los Alamos National
Laboratory/SPL; 53 C; 56 Bettmann/C; 57 CERN/SPL; 58
Mehau Kulyk/SPL; 58-59 Lawrence Berkeley/C; 60t
Tommaso Guicciardini/INFN/SPL; 60b Reuters NewMedia
Inc./C.

Artwork © The Brown Reference Group Ltd

*The Brown Reference Group Ltd has made every effort to
trace copyright holders of the pictures used in this book.
Anyone having claims to ownership not identified above is
invited to contact The Brown Reference Group Ltd.*

CONTENTS

*Page 1: Michael Faraday (left) and John
Frederic Daniell (right).*
This page: Marie and Pierre Curie.

ISAAC NEWTON

1642–1727

" Nature and Nature's Laws lay hid
in Night:
God said, Let Newton be! and All
was Light."

Alexander Pope (1688–1744)
Epitaph written for Newton

ISAAC NEWTON IS WIDELY CONSIDERED TO BE THE
MOST IMPORTANT SCIENTIST OF ALL TIME. HIS
DISCOVERIES, ESPECIALLY THOSE RELATING TO THE
PHYSICS OF LIGHT, MOTION, AND GRAVITY, HAVE
HELPED US TO UNDERSTAND THE UNIVERSE.

Isaac Newton was born in Woolsthorpe, Lincolnshire, on Christmas Day, 1642. In 1661 he went to Trinity College, Cambridge, where he developed a passion for mathematics and astronomy. The university curriculum was based mainly on the ideas of Aristotle, but Newton began to study more modern philosophers, such as the Englishman Francis Bacon (1561–1626) and the Frenchman René Descartes (1596–1650).

In 1665 the Great Plague reached Cambridge, and the university shut. Newton spent the next year at Woolsthorpe developing his theories of color, gravity, and mathematics. By 1669 Newton had become professor of mathematics at Cambridge, and in 1672 he was elected as a member of the Royal Society. In the same year Newton wrote a letter to the Royal Society setting out *A New Theory on Light and Colors,* but it met with criticism, particularly from the eminent physicist Robert Hooke (1635–1703).

THE STRUCTURE OF LIGHT

Newton nevertheless continued his experiments with color. At this time, scientists thought that color was something that occurred when light passed through a substance. Newton was intrigued by what happened when light passes through prisms—triangular blocks of glass. When light rays pass between substances of different densities, like air and water, they change direction. This is called refraction. It is refraction that makes a stick half in and half out of water appear bent.

In 1672 Newton passed a beam of light through a prism onto a screen. As the light traveled through the prism it fanned out into the colors of the spectrum—the colors in a rainbow, ranging from red to violet. Newton showed that if a beam from a single color from the spectrum—red, for example—passed through a second prism, this light remained red. When the second prism was replaced with a lens and the colors of the spectrum passed through this, they turned to white light again.

This 19th-century painting recreates the moment that Newton, sitting in the garden at Woolsthorpe Manor, first wondered whether the force that causes apples to fall is the same as the one that keeps the Moon orbiting around the Earth.

Newton's family home at Woolsthorpe Manor, Lincolnshire, is still very much as it was in Newton's time.

KEY DATES

1661	Admitted into Trinity College, Cambridge
1672	Publishes *A New Theory on Light and Colors*
1687	*The Mathematical Principles of Natural Philosophy*, known as the *Principia*, describes Newton's theory of planetary motion
1693	Suffers nervous breakdown
1696	Appointed warden of Royal Mint in London; becomes master of the Mint in 1699
1703	Elected president of the Royal Society, London
1704	Major work on light and color, *Opticks*, published
1705	Knighted by Queen Anne to become Sir Isaac Newton

Newton concluded that white light was the result of combining all the colors of the spectrum. He found that every color in the spectrum has a different degree of refraction. We now know that this is because light is made up of waves. Each color band has a unique range of wavelengths, and each color band is always refracted the same amount by a prism. Red light, for instance, has a longer wavelength than violet light, and so is refracted less.

Newton's views on the nature of light were challenged by those who favored the wave theory of light, but he pointed out that while we know that sound waves can bend because we hear a bell ringing from the other side of a hill, light does not do this—the hill prevents us from seeing the tower in which the bell is ringing. In fact, we now know that light sometimes behaves like particles and sometimes like waves. Newton was angered by criticism, and he refused to publish anything more. Not until 1704 did the results of his work on light and color appear, in his book *Opticks*. Meanwhile, he turned to attention to how things move.

MOVEMENT AND FORCES

Questions about motion had puzzled thinkers for centuries, but no one had bettered Aristotle's theory that things move because they are pushed or pulled by something or someone—a "mover." French philosopher Jean Buridan (c. 1300-1385) had proposed the idea of impetus, which he saw as a driving force imparted to the object by the mover, to explain why objects carried on moving until halted by friction or air resistance.

Newton rejected these theories, asserting that: "... everything remains naturally in the state in which it is, unless interrupted by an outside force." This tendency is known as "inertia." An object at rest remains at rest until something or someone moves it. Newton applied the same reasoning to moving objects. An object moving in a straight line cannot stop, change direction, speed up, or slow down of its own accord. An outside force is required to influence it.

What are these outside forces? An object will cease moving if a solid obstacle is placed in its path, while friction and air resistance will end the movement of objects propelled through the air. Newton argued that,

if you could remove friction and air resistance, an object set in motion will continue moving. It is inertia that keeps the object in motion until a greater force acts upon it. If he been able to observe movement in the vacuum of space, he would have seen his theory proved.

THE THREE LAWS OF MOTION

Newton formulated three laws of motion, which he wrote up in 1687. The first states that a moving object continues to move at a steady speed in a straight line, or if at rest continues to stay at rest, unless interrupted. The second law states that when a force is applied to an object it accelerates in a straight line in the direction of the force. The object's acceleration (the rate of change in its velocity) depends on its mass (the amount of matter it contains). Newton's third law maintains that if an object exerts force on another object (the action), then that second object exerts an equal but opposite force back (the reaction).

In the 20th century it was discovered that Newton's laws of motion do not apply in quantum mechanics (the

NEWTON IN SPACE

The launching of a space rocket involves all Newton's laws of motion. The engines must overcome the inertia of the rocket (as stated in his first law) and the pull of gravity. As described in his third law, the burning fuel in the engines produces equal and opposite reactions, the force of the expelled gases providing thrust to lift the rocket (right). This law is also demonstrated in an illustration from an 18th-century textbook on Newton (below). Newton's second law notes that the less the mass of the object, the greater the acceleration. The rocket loses mass as it burns fuel and so accelerates accumulatively.

The principle that to every action there is an equal and opposite reaction is also shown by the toy known as Newton's cradle (left). If one ball is swung against the others, only one ball will rise on the other side; if two balls are set in motion, two of the balls opposite will rise, and so on.

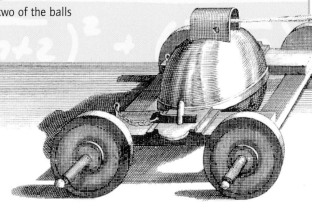

Expanding gas exerts equal force in all directions. Equal resistance from the container stops any movement

With the resistance removed in one direction, the opposing force pushes the vessel forward

physics of very small-scale or high-speed particles and atoms), although they hold for objects at normal speeds.

SOME ASTRONOMICAL PROBLEMS SOLVED

In 1609 Johannes Kepler (1571–1630) showed that the planets move in elliptical orbits. The planets move fastest when at their closest to the Sun, and slowest when farthest away. It was assumed that such changes in speed were caused by the Sun. In 1684 Newton was asked by the astronomer Edmond Halley (1656–1742) to discover what held the planets in orbit. Newton claimed to have the answer. In 1687 he published his proof as *The Mathematical Principles of Natural Philosophy*, or the *Principia*. The book described the workings of the universe with mathematical precision.

Newton stated that there was only one force at work—a force of attraction (what we call the force of gravitation). Newton showed that it governs all motion, in space or on Earth. All matter in the universe attracts all other matter. Gravitation depends only upon the masses of the bodies involved and on the distance between them. All other factors can be ignored.

Newton said that the theory had come to him in the orchard of his home in 1666. He watched an apple fall, and realized that the power of gravity that brought the apple down need not be limited to any particular distance from the Earth but might extend much farther. "Why not as high as the Moon?", he is supposed to have asked. Newton realized that just as the Earth's gravitational pull makes an apple fall to the ground, so it attracts the Moon and keeps it in orbit.

As Newton showed by his first law of motion, if the Earth were not there then the Moon would move through space in a straight line and at a steady speed.

However, a balance is achieved between the Moon being pulled toward the Earth by Earth's gravity and the Moon's forward motion along its path. This deflects the Moon sideways and keeps it in orbit around the Earth.

As with the Earth and Moon, so with the Sun and the planets. Newton argued that the force between two bodies varies depending on their mass and the distance between them. He said that the attractive force of gravity increases with mass and weakens with distance, according to an "inverse square" law. For example, a planet twice as far away as another would be pulled with a quarter of the force. This inverse square law allowed Newton to prove mathematically what Kepler had observed, that the planets move in elliptical orbits.

Comets provided further support for Newton's theory. They had seemed to appear suddenly and unpredictably, flashing quickly across the heavens, never to be seen again. However, Newton and Halley suspected that comets, like planets, move around the Sun in elliptical orbits. Because comets travel in larger orbits, they are seen less frequently from Earth, but Newton and Halley were sure that their orbits would prove to be as predictable as those of the planets.

Gottfried Wilhelm Leibniz
1646–1716

German philosopher and mathematician Gottfried Leibniz was a highly original thinker who made important contributions across an extraordinary range of subjects: science, history, law, philosophy, politics, and theology. He invented a calculating machine; he also constructed a vision of a cosmos made up of simple, indestructible elements called monads. His theory of infinitesimal calculus was published in 1684, prompting a long-running dispute with Newton. His essays on theology placed faith in enlightenment and reason, a view satirized by the French writer Voltaire (1694–1778), who represented this view in *Candide* as the belief that "all is for the best in the best of all possible worlds."

In 1682 Halley tracked the path of a comet across the sky and checked it against records of comets seen in 1531 and 1607. All three paths were very similar, and Halley decided that each occurrence was the same comet coming close to Earth on its orbit round the Sun. He predicted, correctly, that the comet would return in 1758–59. It was named "Halley's Comet" in his honor.

PROBLEMS OF THE ETHER

Many could not understand how gravity could act over vast distances in space; even Newton could not explain it properly. He was coming to believe in the existence of the ether, or quintessence, filling all of space. This was the transparent universal medium believed in by many philosophers. Helpful though such a medium might be to Newton's problem, it also raised new questions. If, for example, the ether was sturdy enough to transmit gravitational forces, it would surely offer resistance to the movement of the planets, slowing them down.

Newton (seated at back) is shown presiding at a meeting of the Royal Society in this 19th-century drawing.

In spite of experiments by Newton to test the existence of the ether, belief in this medium did not disappear until the 19th century when physicists Albert Michelson (1852–1931) and Edward Morley (1838–1923) proved it did not exist in the course of experiments to find how the motion of the Earth affects light waves.

A MATHEMATICAL GENIUS

Newton's discoveries were based on his superb grasp of mathematics. He calculated the area under a hyperbola to 55 decimal places. Mathematicians before Newton were unable to deal with a particular sort of algebraic problem where the answer was not a whole number. In 1676 Newton published a formula that allowed all such values to be worked out. Newton's major contribution, however, was his development of an early form of the

A stern-faced Newton is shown in classical style on this English coin. Newton's post at the Royal Mint was essentially honorary, although he oversaw the introduction of new coinage, and zealously acted to reduce counterfeiting measures.

calculus, the branch of mathematics dealing with continually changing quantities.

Newton's mathematical skills were put to the test in 1696 when the Swiss mathematician Jean Bernoulli (1667–1748) delivered a challenge to solve a particular problem within six months. Newton received the problem at 4 o'clock in the afternoon. He had solved it by 4 o'clock the following morning.

PUBLIC SERVICE

Newton wished to see his career marked by appointment to a significant public position. In 1696 he secured the post of warden at the Royal Mint, the body responsible for producing English coins and medals. He remained at the Mint for the rest of his life, being promoted to master in 1699. In Newton's time people often clipped pieces of silver from coins, and counterfeiting (forging false coins) was also common. To avoid these problems, it was decided to put new coins with milled or grooved edges into circulation. Newton oversaw the change from the old to the new coinage; he also took a leading role in the campaign against counterfeiters. Newton carried out his duties with ruthless efficiency: in 1697 alone, 19 counterfeiters were executed under his orders.

Newton served two terms as an English member of Parliament, and was elected president of the Royal Society in 1703. He was knighted in 1705 by Queen Anne for his public duties. In the last years of his life he published further editions of his principal works, with some additions and alterations, but he did not undertake any major new scientific work.

"If I have seen further [than others]," Newton once said, "it is by standing on the shoulders of giants."

ISAAC NEWTON

SCIENTIFIC BACKGROUND

Before 1660

Greek philosopher Aristotle (384–322 BC) argues that things on Earth move when pushed or pulled by a "mover"

German astronomer Johannes Kepler (1571–1630) publishes his first two laws of planetary motion in *The New Astronomy* (1609), revealing that planets move in elliptical paths

Italian mathematician, physicist, and astronomer Galileo Galilei (1564–1642) publishes his *Discourses upon Two New Sciences* (1638), in which he presents his laws of motion and friction, contradicting many of Aristotle's assertions

French philosopher René Descartes (1596–1650) sets out his view of the cosmos in *Principles of Philosophy* (1644)

1662 The Royal Society in London is granted its royal charter

1665–66 Newton develops ideas on calculus, light and optics, and gravity

1668 Newton invents the reflecting telescope

1672 English physicist Robert Hooke (1635–1703) suggests a "wave" theory of light

1675 English astronomer John Flamsteed (1646–1719) is appointed astronomer-royal at the Greenwich Observatory in London, England by King Charles II (1630–1685)

1679 Hooke suggests that gravitational force might operate according to an "inverse-square" law of attraction, leading to a later dispute with Newton

1684 German philosopher and mathematician Gottfried von Leibniz (1646–1716) invents calculus, a branch of mathematics, prompting a long-running argument with Newton

1687 Newton presents his three laws of planetary motion and his law of universal gravitation in his groundbreaking book, the *Principia*

(1660)   (1670)   (1680)

POLITICAL AND CULTURAL BACKGROUND

1665 The New Jersey colony is founded by English colonists, who make Elizabethtown their capital

1675 Work begins on St. Paul's Cathedral in London, England. It is designed by English architect, inventor, astronomer, and gifted mathematician Christopher Wren (1632–1723)

1682 English religious nonconformist William Penn (1644–1718), member of the Society of Friends (Quakers), is granted land in North America by King Charles II to establish a Quaker colony; the territory is called Pennsylvania

1683 William Penn signs the Great Treaty of Shackamaxon, by which the Delaware Native Americans grant him vast territories

1690 Dutch physicist Christiaan Huygens (1629–1695) publishes his theory of gravity in *Discourse on the Cause of Gravity*

1690 Huygens publishes his *Treatise on Light*, which has been almost complete since 1678. In it he explains reflection and refraction, and puts forward his wave or pulse theory of light

1704 Newton rejects the wave theory of light, presenting his work on light and color in his book *Opticks*

1705 English astronomer Edmond Halley (1656–1742) applies Newton's ideas to comets, correctly predicting the return of one—later to be called "Halley's comet"—on its orbit around the Sun

1712 In the wake of strong pressure from Newton, Flamsteed's star catalogs—charting the position of nearly 3,000 stars—are published without his permission. Newton uses the data for his lunar theory

1720 After Flamsteed's death, Halley becomes astronomer-royal at the Greenwich Observatory

1724 Tsar Peter the Great (1672–1725) founds the Academy of Sciences in St. Petersburg, Russia

After 1730

1748 Swiss mathematician Leonhard Euler (1707–1783) publishes *Introduction to Infinitesimal Analysis*; later produces textbooks on differential and integral calculus

1905, 1915 German-American physicist Albert Einstein (1879–1955) presents his special and general theories of relativity (1905 and 1915), in which he revises aspects of Newton's laws on motion and gravity

1690 1700 1710 1720 1730

1690 William III of England (1650–1702) completes the Protestant conquest of Ireland when he defeats the Catholic ex-king of England, James II (1633–1701), at the Battle of the Boyne

1690 The English philosopher John Locke (1632–1704) produces his *Two Treatises of Civil Government*, which supports natural law above the authority of a ruling body

1697 Tsar Peter the Great of Russia (1672–1725) visits Europe unannounced; the trip encourages him to Westernize his own country

1703 Tsar Peter the Great founds St. Petersburg, the new capital city, on the northwest coast of Russia

1710 The Royal Chapel at Versailles, designed by Jules Hardouin Mansart (1645–1708), chief architect to French king Louis XIV (1638–1715), is completed

1715 The first performance of the Water Music by Handel (1685–1759) takes place on the River Thames in London, England

1715 Louis XV (1710–1774), known as "Louis the Well-Beloved," is crowned king in France

1719 *Robinson Crusoe* by Daniel Defoe (1660–1731) is the first known English novel. Based on a true story, it describes the life of a man wrecked on a remote island

1726 English writer and clergyman Jonathan Swift (1667–1745) completes his satire on politics, *Gulliver's Travels*. Among the characters that Lemuel Gulliver meets are the inhabitants of Lilliput, who are only six inches high

1732 American statesman and scientist Benjamin Franklin (1706–1790) begins publication of *Poor Richard's Almanac*, which gains a vast circulation in the American colonies

MICHAEL FARADAY

1791–1867

"There is no honor too great to pay to the memory of Michael Faraday— one of the greatest scientific discoverers of all time."

Ernest Rutherford (1871–1937)
New Zealand born British physicist

PERHAPS THE GREATEST EXPERIMENTAL PHYSICIST OF ALL TIME, FARADAY IS FAMOUS FOR HIS WORK IN ELECTROMAGNETISM (THE PHYSICAL EFFECTS THAT MAGNETISM AND ELECTRICITY HAVE UPON EACH OTHER). HE ALSO DISCOVERED THE LAWS OF ELECTROLYSIS, AND MADE EARLY TYPES OF ELECTRIC MOTORS, DYNAMOS, AND TRANSFORMERS.

Michael Faraday had only a scant education. However, he was apprenticed to a London bookbinder and learned much—especially about science—from the books he bound. In fact he yearned for a career in science. He attended lectures at the City Philosophical Society, a self-improvement society, and taught himself about electricity. In 1812 Faraday attended lectures at the Royal Institution, a body aimed at sharing scientific information, given by the great scientist Sir Humphry Davy (1778–1829). Later, Davy needed a temporary assistant, and Faraday was recommended. In 1813 Davy offered Faraday the job of laboratory assistant at the Royal Institution.

The following year Faraday accompanied Davy on a tour of Europe, where they met leading scientists, including French physicist André Ampère (1775–1836) and Italian physicist Alessandro Volta (1745–1827). Both men would later make important discoveries in electromagnetism. Back in London, in 1825 Faraday became director of the Royal Institution laboratory, and he was made professor of chemistry in 1833. By then he had begun his electrical experiments.

EARLY STUDIES IN ELECTRICITY

The word "electricity" comes from the Greek word "electron," meaning amber. When amber is rubbed it becomes charged with "static" electricity, which attracts fluff and feathers. Because static electricity could attract things, people thought that magnetism and electricity might be related in some way, but were not sure how.

The first major advance came in 1746 when the Dutch physicist Peter van Musschenbroek (1692–1761) invented what became known as the Leiden jar. This was a glass jar coated inside and out with metal. A chain ran from the lid into the jar; when the lid was linked to a friction machine an electric charge passed

Faraday in the laboratory at the Royal Institution, London. On the right is the apparatus for his electrical experiments.

through the chain into the jar and was then passed to the metal coating and was stored. This type of storage device is known as a capacitor. People who touched the jar when it was charged up would receive a shock.

American Benjamin Franklin (1706–1790) carried out experiments to determine the nature of electricity. Electricity was known to attract and repel, and Franklin devised the term "positive" for its attractive force and "negative" for its repulsive force. His discovery that lightning is an electric charge led him to suggest a practical way of protecting buildings by proposing that metal rods, or lightning conductors, should be attached to draw the electric charge from a lightning strike and guide it safely down to the earth.

KEY DATES

1804	Apprenticed as a bookbinder
1812	Appointed laboratory assistant to Humphry Davy at the Royal Institution, London
1813	Accompanies Davy on European tour
1821	Establishes existence of electromagnetic rotation. Marries Sarah Barnard
1825	Appointed director of the Royal Institution laboratory
1827	Begins children's Christmas lectures at the Royal Institution
1831	Demonstrates electromagnetic induction
1833	Establishes two laws of electrolysis

In 1800 Alessandro Volta built a "voltaic pile," or battery (see below). The battery created a continuous flow of electrical charge called a "current." Later, two English chemists, William Nicholson (1753-1815) and Anthony Carlisle (1768-1840), found that a battery can split water into hydrogen and oxygen. When two metal plates, attached to the positive and negative sides of the battery, were suspended in water, gas bubbles appeared. The scientists collected the gas gathering above the plates and found that hydrogen gas collected at one plate and oxygen at the other. This process became known as electrolysis (see box opposite).

ELECTROMAGNETISM AND DYNAMOS

Danish physicist Hans Christian Oersted (1777-1851) made the link between magnetism and electricity when, in 1820, he passed an electric current through a wire pointing in a north-south direction. A compass happened to be lying beneath the wire, with its needle aligned in the same direction. As the current passed through the wire the needle turned clockwise for 90 degrees so that it was at right angles to the wire. When the compass was placed above the wire, the needle deviated 90 degrees in the opposite direction. Oersted realized that the

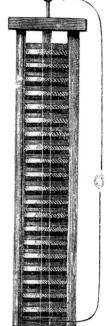

Zinc

Silver

Pad soaked in salt water

The voltaic pile has alternate disks of zinc, silver, and a wet pad. A chemical reaction between the disks causes an electric charge to flow along a copper wire running from the top silver disk to the bottom zinc disk.

Benjamin Franklin proved that lightning and electricity are the same force. The wet string on a kite conducted electricity from a thunderstorm to charge a capacitor.

magnetic effect of the electricity was moving the needle. This is known as electromagnetism.

In 1821 Faraday made a wire rotate continuously by electromagnetism. He had converted electrical movement into mechanical movement, inventing the first electric motor. Then in 1831 he created the apparatus that allowed him to find "electrical induction." Faraday wound a coil of insulated wire connected to a battery around one side of an iron ring. He wound a second coil of wire around the opposite side of the ring, and ran the wires to an instrument for measuring electrical currents. When he switched the current on, it flowed through the first wire. This magnetized the iron ring and caused a current to flow through the second coil. The same thing happened when the current was switched off, because current only

A SILVER LINING

Electrolysis is a process in which an electric current splits chemical compounds into their elements. One piece of metal is attached to the negative electrode (cathode) of a battery and the other to the positive (anode). An electrode is an electrical conductor. The pieces of metal are placed in a dish containing a liquid that can conduct electricity; this is called the "electrolyte." The molecules in the electrolyte split into positive and negative particles called ions; positive ions are attracted to the cathode and negative ions to the anode. The process had important industrial applications. Metals could be extracted from their ores. Cheap metals could be coated with a thin layer of silver: this was known as "electroplating," or "silver plating."

Faraday established two laws of electrolysis. The first is that the ability to break down compounds is proportional to the amount of electricity passing through them. The second law allowed chemists to calculate how much electricity was needed to deliver a precise amount of silver to the cathode.

In silver-plating, the positive electrode (anode) is silver, the electrolyte is silver nitrate, and an object made of a cheaper metal (such as zinc) is connected to the negative terminal (cathode). When the current flows, the positively charged ions—the silver—are attracted to the cathode, and the metal object becomes coated in silver.

Spoons are lowered into a tank ready for silver-plating. Faraday's laws made it possible to calculate accurately the amount of electricity needed in order to carry out electroplating in the most cost-effective manner.

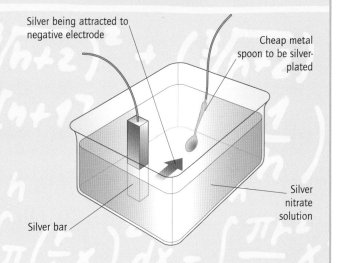

Silver being attracted to negative electrode

Cheap metal spoon to be silver-plated

Silver nitrate solution

Silver bar

flows when a magnetic field varies or moves (by being switched on or off, for instance). Faraday called these bursts of current "induced." He produced the same effect by moving a magnet in and out of a coil of wire. Faraday described this as a "conversion of magnetism to electricity"; it was the first dynamo, a device that

This huge battery, using 2,000 double plates of zinc and copper, was built at the Royal Institution in 1807. Davy and Faraday used it for electrolysis and other experiments.

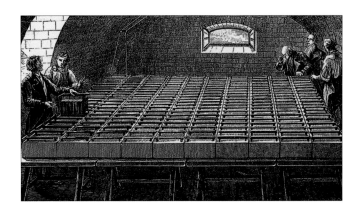

converts mechanical energy to electrical energy. He also found that by rotating a copper disk between the poles of an electromagnet, a steady current was produced; in other words, rotary motion had become electricity.

Faraday had established that "electricity, whatever may be its source, is identical in its nature" by showing that different forms of electricity all behave in similarly predictable ways.

FARADAY'S FIELD THEORY

Faraday went on to develop field theory, based on the concept of lines of force. He imagined that there must be lines of force spreading out from centers of force, and that connections could be drawn between them. Later Faraday devised an experiment to prove that these lines exist. Sprinkling iron filings on some paper, he held a magnet underneath. The lines of force could be clearly seen. He also thought that all physical and chemical activities are interrelated, and that magnetism had an influence on all objects.

In 1845 Faraday showed that light could be affected by magnetism, confirming his faith in the unity of forces. He was less successful in his attempts to link gravity and electricity. He tried frequently to prove the link, but failing health and memory ended his scientific career in the 1860s. It was James Clerk Maxwell (1831–1879), a Scottish physicist, who developed Faraday's ideas into a mathematically sound theory in his *Treatise on Electricity and Magnetism* (1873).

FARADAY'S LEGACY

Faraday sowed the seeds of a new electrical industry, though batteries that could drive big motors were heavy and expensive, so in transport the steam engine was still a more efficient method of power. Electric trains were produced, but they were very slow. Dynamos provided a useful source of electrical power, first in the electroplating industry. Electrical lighting was initially provided by arc lamps. They produced a "continuous spark" between two carbon rods, but gas lamps were still preferred by many people. By the 1880s the development of efficient generators, such as steam turbines, meant that electricity could be produced on a much greater scale than before. At the same time, the

Faraday lecturing at the Royal Institution. Prince Albert, husband of Queen Victoria, and two of their four sons are seated at center front.

invention of the incandescent light bulb by American physicist Thomas Edison (1847–1931) in 1879 brought about a breakthrough in electric lighting.

Faraday's entire career was spent at the Royal Institution. It developed a program to encourage many aspects of science. Practical projects included the invention of the miners' safety lamp known as the Davy Lamp, and advising the government on the purity of the water supply. Faraday played a key role in the

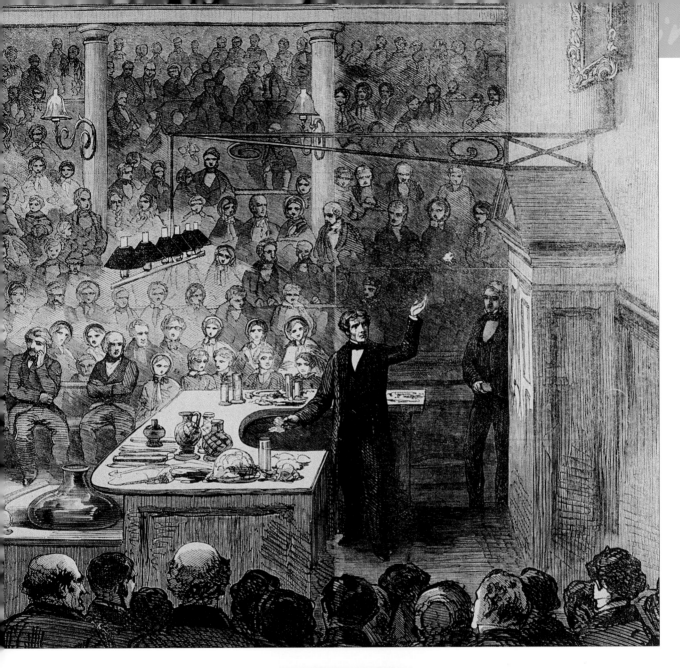

Institution's efforts to popularize science, starting the Christmas lectures for children in 1827. The aim was to make the lectures entertaining as well as instructive, and great emphasis was placed on practical demonstrations.

Faraday became the most famous scientist in Britain, but he refused to accept any official public post. His health began to fail for a second time after 1855, and he was forced to give up any experimental work. He became forgetful and confused; he may have developed Alzheimer's disease.

Faraday and his wife belonged to the Sandemanian Church, which believed that it was against the word of the Bible to accumulate riches and pursue worldly reward. For this reason, Faraday turned down the offer of a knighthood from the English queen Victoria (1819-1901). This was a high honor, given in recognition of his services to science, but he preferred to remain "plain Mr Faraday to the end."

An early photograph showing Michael Faraday and his wife, Sarah.

MICHAEL FARADAY

SCIENTIFIC BACKGROUND

Before 1800

Dutch physicist Peter van Musschenbroek (1692–1761) invents the Leiden jar, which stores an electrical charge

Italian physiologist Luigi Galvani (1737–1798) claims to have discovered "animal electricity"

American-born scientist Benjamin Thompson (later Count Rumford) (1753–1814) founds the Royal Institution in London

1800 Italian physicist Alessandro Volta (1745–1827) invents the electric battery; water is decomposed into hydrogen and oxygen

1807 English physicist and physician Thomas Young (1773–1829) revives the wave theory of light first proposed by English scientist Robert Hooke (1635–1703) and Dutch physicist and mathematician Christiaan Huygens (1629–1695)

1808 English scientist Humphry Davy (1778–1829) connects battery wires to two carbon rods to create the "arc lamp"

1816 Scottish physicist and inventor David Brewster (1781–1868) invents the kaleidoscope

1820 Danish physicist Hans Christian Oersted (1777–1851) demonstrates the magnetic effect of an electric current

1821 Faraday establishes existence of electromagnetic rotation

1825 Faraday discovers benzene

1827 German physicist Georg Simon Ohm (1789–1854) publishes Ohm's Law, which describes the relationship between electrical current, voltage, and resistance

---

(1800)   **(1810)**   **(1820)**

POLITICAL AND CULTURAL BACKGROUND

1801 Virginia lawyer Thomas Jefferson (1743–1826), who drafted the Declaration of Independence in 1776, becomes third president of the United States

1808 Napoleon's brother Joseph Bonaparte (1768–1844) seizes the Spanish throne; despite continued opposition from his subjects, he will reign until 1813

1818 The border between Canada and the United States is fixed

1821 Nationalist Greeks begin their battle for independence from the Turkish Ottoman Empire; a Greek kingdom is eventually established in 1832

1822 The German folklorists Jacob Ludwig Carl Grimm (1785–1863) and his brother Wilhelm Carl Grimm (1786–1859) complete the third volume of their collection of folk stories, *Grimm's Fairy Tales*

1827 American bird artist John James Audubon (1785–1851) begins publication of *Birds of America*, which will eventually consist of more than 1,000 lifesize drawings

1830 American scientist Joseph Henry (1797–1878) discovers electromagnetic induction, but does not publish his work immediately

1831 Faraday demonstrates electromagnetic induction

1833 Faraday establishes two laws of electrolysis

1835 Faraday describes "Faraday rotation," or how polarized light is rotated in a magnetic field

1844 Faraday describes his force-field theory—that a web of lines of gravitational force spreads out from the Sun and runs throughout the universe—in a lecture at the Royal Institution

1845 Irish-born Scottish physicist and mathematician William Thomson, Lord Kelvin (1824–1907), gives a mathematical explanation for "lines of force"

1859 German chemist Robert Bunsen (1811–1899) and German physicist Gustav Kirchhoff (1824–1887) determine that the light emitted from glowing substances when passed through a prism is unique to each substance; this heralded the science of spectroscopy

1861 Faraday publishes one of his best-known lectures, *The Chemical History of a Candle*, which he has delivered at the Royal Institution

1864 Scottish physicist James Clerk Maxwell (1831–1879) publishes *A Dynamical Theory of the Electromagnetic Field*, which describes the main features of electricity, magnetism, and light in four mathematical equations

1873 Maxwell publishes his *Treatise on Electricity and Magnetism*, which predicts that electromagnetic waves might be generated in a laboratory

1879 American inventor Thomas Alva Edison (1847–1931) invents the incandescent electric light bulb

After 1880

1887 As predicted by Maxwell, German physicist Heinrich Hertz (1857–1894) succeeds in generating electromagnetic waves, which he finds behave like light waves but have different wavelengths

1830	1840	1850	1860	1870

1830 Mormonism is founded in the United States by American religious leader Joseph Smith (1805–1844)

1835 More than 12,000 European-origin South Africans (Afrikaners), protesting at policies under British rule that include a ban on slavery, begin their "Great Trek" northeast from Cape Colony to settle new areas; they later found Transvaal (1852) and the Orange Free State (1854)

1846 The Mexican–American War begins in a dispute over American expansion in Texas; Mexico renounces claims to Texas in 1848

1846 The potato famine in Ireland leads to a massive increase in the numbers of people emigrating from there to the United States over the following two years

1852 After widespread revolution throughout Europe, Louis Napoleon (1808–1873) restores the French empire when he becomes Emperor Napoleon III

1857 Muslim and Hindu troops stage a series of mutinies against British rule in India; these are suppressed, and in 1858 authority in India is transferred from the East India Company to the British monarchy

1867 Russia sells Alaska to American secretary-of-state William Henry Seward (1801–1872); for a time "Seward's Folly" remains uneconomical, until gold is discovered there in 1896

1869 The first American transcontinental railroad runs from Sacramento, California, to Omaha, Nebraska, cutting travel time from San Francisco to New York from a minimum of three months to just eight days

1876 At the Battle of Little Big Horn, a U.S. cavalry force under Lieutenant-Colonel George Armstrong Custer (1839–1876) is massacred by Dakota Sioux led by Tatanka Iyotake, known as Sitting Bull (1834–1890)

MARIE AND PIERRE CURIE

1867–1934 and 1859–1906

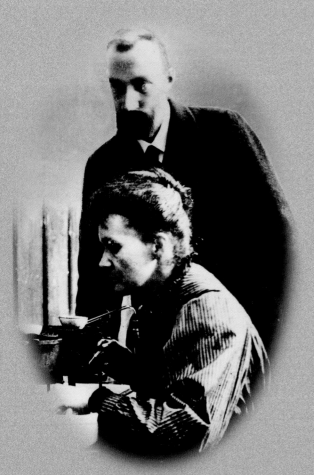

"I am among those who think that science has great beauty.... A scientist in his laboratory is not only a technician but also a child placed in front of natural phenomena that impress him like a fairy tale..."

Marie Curie

MARIE AND PIERRE CURIE WERE PHYSICISTS WHO DISCOVERED THE ELEMENTS POLONIUM AND RADIUM. THEY ALSO PIONEERED THE STUDY OF THE NATURAL FLOW OF ENERGY CALLED RADIATION. MARIE'S THOUGHT THAT RADIATION EMANATES FROM WITHIN THE ATOM ITSELF WAS THE START OF NUCLEAR PHYSICS.

Born Maria Sklodowska in Warsaw on November 7, 1867, Marie Curie was the youngest of five children. Her parents, both teachers, instilled a love of learning into their children. When Marie wanted to find something out she would not stop until she uncovered the truth. Political upheavals caused Marie's parents to lose their jobs, then her eldest sister died of typhus and her mother died two years later. These tragedies overshadowed Marie's childhood, yet she still excelled at school. Further education was not open to women in Poland, so Marie's sister Bronia went to Paris to study medicine, while Marie stayed behind. It was agreed that when Bronia qualified she would help Marie to complete her education.

In 1891 Bronia qualified and married a Polish doctor living in Paris. Marie joined them. She entered the Sorbonne, part of the University of Paris, attended the lectures of leading physicists, and met other scientists. Marie graduated in physical sciences in 1893, and in mathematical sciences in 1894. After her first graduation, Marie worked in a laboratory run by the French physicist Gabriel Lippmann (1845–1921), who later won the 1908 Nobel Prize for physics.

A MEETING AND A MARRIAGE

In 1894 Marie met Pierre Curie, thinking he might be able to help her with her work. Pierre was head of the laboratory at the School of Industrial Physics and Chemistry. After their meeting, Marie was impressed by him, and Pierre was drawn to this woman who shared his love for science. They married on July 25, 1895.

Pierre Curie was born in Paris on May 15, 1859. As a youth, Pierre had been very interested in mathematics

Pierre Curie, seen holding up a glowing sample of radium, was a respected scientist when he met Marie. At first, he was viewed as the more important researcher.

KEY DATES

1877 Pierre graduates from the Sorbonne, part of the University of Paris

1878 Pierre becomes a laboratory assistant at the Sorbonne

1880 Pierre discovers piezoelectricity

1882 Pierre appointed supervisor at the School of Industrial Physics and Chemistry

1891 Marie becomes a student at the Sorbonne

1893 Marie graduates in physical sciences

1894 Marie graduates in mathematical sciences; meets Pierre Curie

1895 Marie and Pierre marry on July 25; Pierre awarded doctorate

1898 Curies discover polonium in July and radium in December

1903 Marie awarded doctorate; Marie and Pierre, together with Antoine Becquerel, are awarded Nobel Prize for physics

1908 Marie made a professor at the Sorbonne

1911 Marie awarded Nobel Prize for chemistry

1918 Marie becomes director of the Radium Institute

1932 Radium Institute opened in Warsaw

1934 Joliot-Curies discover artificial radioactivity

1935 Irène Joliot-Curie and Frédéric Joliot awarded the Nobel Prize for chemistry

MARIE AND PIERRE CURIE

THE DISCOVERY OF X-RAYS

On November 5, 1895, the German physicist Wilhelm Konrad Röntgen (1845–1923), head of the physics department at the University of Würzburg, Germany, was studying how cathode rays (the rays emitted from a negative electrode, see opposite) produced a glow when they fell on a screen coated with certain chemicals. The glow was very faint, so to help him see it, Röntgen blacked out the room and wrapped cardboard around the cathode-ray tube. The tube was pointed at one chemical-coated screen, but when he switched it on he noticed that another screen, also chemically coated but well out of the "line of fire" of the cathode-ray tube, was glowing as well.

When he turned off the tube the glow on the second screen vanished, and when he turned it on again it reappeared. He took the screen into the next room, but found that the screen still glowed if the tube in the other room was switched on. Whatever was causing the glow was coming out of the sides of the tube and passing through cardboard and the wall. Later investigation showed that the rays could even pass through a thin sheet of metal. The rays would also expose a photographic plate so that coins in a wooden box could be photographed. When he placed his wife's hand over a photographic plate and exposed it, the result was an image of the bones of her hand and the ring she had on (see above).

On December 28, 1895, Röntgen wrote a paper describing this mysterious form of radiation. Röntgen called them X-rays, since their source was unknown. We now know that they are electromagnetic rays, emitted when matter is bombarded with fast, negatively charged electrons. On January 23, 1896 Röntgen gave his first public demonstration of X-rays: the audience watched amazed as he X-rayed the hand of the elderly Swiss biologist Rudolf Albert von Kölliker (1817–1905).

Röntgen took this X-ray photograph of his wife's hand, which also shows a ring on her finger (left). X-rays began to interest the public, too; a contemporary postcard (above) imagines an X-ray view of people on the beach.

X-rays in Medicine

Scientists soon realized how useful these penetrating X-rays could be. Physicians could look inside the human body without using surgery. The rays penetrated soft tissue but not bones or denser matter, so could be used to detect bone fractures, or to find bullets or shrapnel lodged in wounded soldiers. Abnormalities in lung tissue also showed up on X-ray photographs. This meant that tuberculosis of the lungs, one of the most dangerous of diseases, could be diagnosed early. Mass screening units were able to take chest X-rays of entire populations.

X-ray equipment was quickly installed in hospitals. It was used in the 1898 Spanish–American war, and more widely in World War I (1914–18). Marie Curie assisted in setting up X-ray equipment for the French, and helped train American medical staff in its use. The dangers of X-rays were not understood at first, and no measures were taken to protect early operators: many suffered cancers or leukemias as a result of

RÖNTGEN

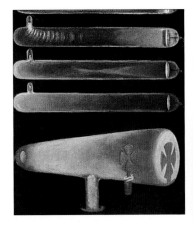

Cathode-ray tubes (right) have an electrode at each end, one positively charged (the anode) and the other negatively charged (the cathode). The cathode glows when an electric current is passed through it. The shadow cast by the Maltese cross in the lower tube made British physicist William Crookes (1832–1919) think that cathode rays travel in straight lines. In 1897 English physicist J. J. Thomson (1856–1940) identified cathode rays as a stream of negatively charged particles, later named electrons.

their exposure to radiation, including Marie Curie and her daughter. Today X-rays are still widely used for screening, diagnosis, and the treatment of disease, but the risks to patients and radiographers have been greatly reduced.

An X-ray machine used in the Boer War (1899–1902). The large apparatus in the background generates electricity, the glass X-ray tube is placed in front, and the fluorescent screen receives the X-ray picture.

and geometry. He graduated from the Sorbonne, and in 1878 he became a laboratory assistant there. That is when he had begun research which led to the discovery of piezoelectricity. Pierre and his brother Jacques (1856–1941) discovered piezoelectricity in 1880. This is the electricity produced by applying stress to certain crystals. They noticed that if some crystals (such as quartz) were compressed or stretched, an electric potential (a difference in charge causing an electric current to flow) appeared across them. Also, if a rapidly changing electric potential were applied to a crystal, the crystal expanded and contracted rhythmically. Today this phenomenon is used in quartz watches or clocks, where the regular oscillation of a quartz crystal ensures that the watch or clock keeps accurate time.

In 1882 Pierre discovered that the magnetic strength of a weakly magnetic substance is related to its temperature. This is known as Curie's Law. He also found that ferromagnetic substances (iron, cobalt, nickel, and certain alloys, which are more magnetic than other known substances) lose their magnetism above a certain critical temperature, now called the Curie Point. Pierre presented his research as a thesis, and in 1895 he was awarded the degree of doctor of science. In 1900 he was appointed a lecturer at the Sorbonne, and in 1904 he was made a professor.

Pierre and Marie with their eldest daughter, Irène (left). The Curies in their laboratory (above).

EXPLORING RADIOACTIVITY

In 1898 French physicist Antoine Becquerel (1852–1908) discovered that the element uranium emitted X-rays, and Marie decided to study this for her doctoral thesis. Radiation "ionizes" the air (charges it electrically), and Marie measured the electric current produced. This was a measure of the intensity of the radiation given off by uranium. She called this emission "radioactivity." She tested uranium compounds (substances in which uranium was combined with other elements) and discovered that the intensity of the radiation increased proportionately to the amount of uranium present. This confirmed Becquerel's discovery that uranium was the source of the radiation. Marie then discovered that another element, thorium, also gave off radiation.

Marie's most important research was with the mineral pitchblende. She discovered that it is more radioactive than can be accounted for by the amount of uranium it contains, and decided that it must have traces of another radioactive substance. The Curies set about identifying it. By July 1898, they had discovered the new radioactive element. Marie named it polonium.

Stripped of its uranium and polonium, the pitchblende was still radioactive. The Curies realized that it must contain something else, and by 1898 they had found this element, too, and named it radium. Marie wondered where the radiation was coming from; she thought it might be caused by tiny particles inside the atoms. But it was left to Ernest Rutherford to discover that the atom did indeed consist of a central nucleus surrounded by orbiting electrons.

In 1903 Marie received a doctorate for her research into pitchblende. In the same year she and

A NEW FORCE OF NATURE

In 1896, when Röntgen announced his discovery that X-rays make certain substances fluoresce, or glow, Antoine Henri Becquerel (1852–1908), professor of physics at the École Polytechnique in Paris, was intrigued. Becquerel came from a long line of physicists: his grandfather Antoine César Becquerel (1788–1878) was the first person to use electrolysis to separate metals from their ores, and his father, Alexandre Edmond Becquerel (1820–1891), researched into solar radiation. Antoine Henri Becquerel was an expert on fluorescence.

Fluorescence is a form of luminiscence (the emission of nonthermal, or heatless, light) in which certain substances exposed to light radiation at one wavelength emit light of another wavelength, or color. Unlike phosphorescence, the light disappears almost instantly. Fluorescence is seen in the "dayglo" jackets that make emergency workers brightly visible, and phosphorescence is used in the coating on the back of TV screens.

Röntgen had shown that X-rays could penetrate materials that visible light cannot. So in February 1896 Antoine Becquerel wrapped a photographic plate in black paper, placed some crystals of a fluorescing substance on it, and exposed it to bright sunshine. When he developed the plate he found there was an image of the crystals on it. He assumed that the crystals had absorbed the Sun's energy and emitted it as X-rays, which had then penetrated the black paper.

He prepared to repeat the experiment, but the weather turned cloudy, so he put the wrapped plate, with the same crystals on top, in a drawer. March came, and the weather was still cloudy. Becquerel grew impatient and decided to develop the plate anyway. To his surprise, the silhouette of the crystals—along with the outline of a piece of metal that had been pushed underneath them—"appeared with great intensity" on the photographic plate. This meant that the crystals must have emitted radiation without having been exposed to any external source of energy—something quite different from fluorescence.

Becquerel then turned his attention to the radiation itself. He found that it penetrated materials and that it also ionized air (made it electrically charged), as do X-rays. The crystals emitted radiation in an endless stream and in all directions. At first, this radiation was called "Becquerel Rays," but in 1898 Marie Curie gave the process the name that we use today: radioactivity.

The crystals that Becquerel used in his experiment were potassium uranyl sulfate, a compound containing uranium. Becquerel discovered that the radiation was coming from the uranium. It was this experiment that inspired Marie Curie to study uranium. But it was not until the Curies identified other radioactive elements such as thorium and polonium that it was clear some new force of nature had been discovered.

In 1899 Becquerel discovered that the radiation could be deflected by a magnetic field, showing that it must consist at least partly of charged particles. By measuring the extent of the deflection, he concluded that the particles were electrons, identical to those in cathode rays, which had first been identified by J. J. Thomson in 1897.

Antoine Becquerel shared the 1903 Nobel Prize for physics with the Curies for his work on radioactivity.

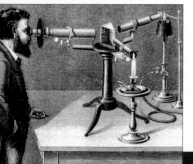

Spectroscopes like this model (left) dispersed electromagnetic radiation to form a spectrum, so each element could be identified (below).

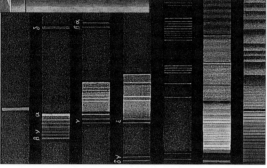

Pierre were awarded the Davy Medal of the Royal Society in London and, with Antoine Becquerel, the Nobel Prize for physics.

CARRYING ON DESPITE TRAGEDY

On April 9, 1906 Pierre collapsed under a horse-drawn wagon—probably because he was weak as a result of radiation sickness—and died. But Marie completed their research. On May 13 she took over Pierre's professorship at the Sorbonne, and in 1908 she was made a professor. In 1911 she was awarded the Nobel Prize for chemistry for discovering polonium and radium, and for isolating radium. When war broke out in 1914, Marie helped to install X-ray equipment into ambulances and drove them to the front lines. The Red Cross made her head of its radiological service.

The Curies refused to patent their discoveries, and invested their money in research. Therefore Marie remained poor for most of her life. It had been decided before the war to create a Radium Institute to examine the properties and medical uses of radioactive elements. When the institute opened in 1918, Marie became its director, and her eldest daughter, Irène, joined the staff. In 1925 the French physicist Frédéric Joliot (1900–1958) became a special assistant to Marie. Irène and Frédéric were married in 1926 and took the surname Joliot-Curie.

A second Radium Institute was opened in 1932 in Warsaw, with Marie's sister, Bronia, as director. By this time Marie's health was failing. The substance that would save so many lives had made her ill. Marie Curie died on July 4, 1934, from the blood disease leukemia.

A FINE LEGACY

Irène and Frédéric Joliot-Curie continued researching. In 1934 they bombarded aluminum with alpha particles (two protons and two neutrons). This produces protons by knocking them out of the aluminum atoms. They found that after the bombardment, although no more protons were produced, they still detected a form of radiation. The source of the radiation was phosphorus, formed from aluminum as a result of the alpha radiation. It was an unstable form, known as a radioactive isotope, and was emitting beta-radiation.

The Joliot-Curies had discovered artificial radioactivity. This showed that it is possible artificially to produce radioactive isotopes of any element. For this discovery Frédéric and Irène Joliot-Curie were awarded the 1935 Nobel Prize for chemistry.

Ernest Rutherford
1871–1937

Ernest Rutherford, the founder of nuclear physics, was born in Brightwater, New Zealand. In 1895 he won a scholarship to Cambridge University, England. In 1898 he became professor of physics at McGill University, Canada. Here he studied radiation emissions and, with English radiochemist Frederick Soddy (1877–1956), formulated the laws of radioactive decay in 1905. He published his nuclear model of the atom in 1911. In 1919 he became professor of physics and director of the Cavendish laboratory at Cambridge University. He changed nitrogen atoms into oxygen by bombarding them with alpha particles, and in 1920 he predicted the existence of a subatomic particle called the neutron. He was awarded the Nobel Prize for chemistry in 1908.

Frédéric Joliot-Curie (right), worked without protection in his laboratory before the dangers of radiation were realized.

During World War II (1939–45) the Joliot-Curies worked with the French Resistance. But Frédéric and Irène were communists, and after the war they were regarded with suspicion by the authorities. Frédéric was director of scientific research and commissioner of the French atomic energy program (1946–50), but was dismissed from his post due to his political sympathies at the start of the Cold War. Irène died from leukemia on March 17, 1956, and Frédéric died of the same disease two years later.

RADIATION TREATMENTS

In the early years of the 20th century radioactive substances were believed to be beneficial. People thought that they could be used as a tonic to invigorate the body, or that bath salts, containing radium, would give out soothing rays in a warm bath. Scientists also saw that radium might have medical benefits. Frederick Soddy (1877-1956) suggested inhaling it as a cure for tuberculosis. Tiny amounts of radium were inserted beneath the skin to treat diseased tissue.

It soon became evident that radium could harm as well as heal. Radiation can halt the spread of cancer when applied to diseased cells, and sometimes cure it. But it also destroys healthy cells, with fatal results. It therefore has to be used very carefully. Radium is still used to treat some cancers, but in tiny amounts that are applied very precisely. X-rays and gamma rays are also used to treat cancers deep inside the body.

MARIE AND PIERRE CURIE

Before 1895

The German mathematician and physicist Julius Plücker (1801–1868) observes that electrical discharge in a high-vacuum tube causes a fluorescent glow that can be moved by an electromagnet

The English physicist William Crookes (1832–1919) invents the evacuated glass "Crookes tube," which produces the stream of energy known as "cathode rays"

1895 The German physicist Wilhelm Röntgen (1845–1923) discovers X-rays

1896 The French physicist Antoine Becquerel (1852–1908) records radiation from uranium

1896–98 Marie and Pierre Curie discover two new elements: polonium and radium

1897 The English physicist J. J. Thomson (1856–1940) shows that cathode rays are made up of negatively charged particles; they are named "electrons"

1899 British physicist Ernest Rutherford (1871–1937) discovers alpha and beta particles

1900 The French physicist Paul-Ulrich Villard (1860–1934) discovers gamma rays

1903 Rutherford and the English chemist Frederick Soddy (1877–1956) establish laws of radioactive decay and transformation

1903 The Curies and Becquerel jointly win the Nobel Prize for physics

1908 To measure radiation, Rutherford and the German physicist Hans Geiger (1882–1945) invent the Geiger counter

1895   1900   1905

1895 In Paris, brothers Auguste (1862–1954) and Louis (1864–1948) Lumière show motion pictures on screen for the first time

1896 The Klondike gold rush starts in Canada's Yukon Territory

1900 In China, the anti-Christian "Boxers" (League of Righteous Harmonious Fists) wage a violent revolt against foreign influence

1901 In Buffalo, New York, President William McKinley (1843–1901) is assassinated by the Polish-American anarchist Leon Czolgosz (1873–1901)

1904 Construction begins on the Panama Canal, which by 1916 will allow shipping to pass between the Atlantic and Pacific oceans

1905 Revolution sweeps Russia after humiliating defeats in wars with Japan. Tsar Nicholas II (1868–1918) is forced to create a Duma (parliament)

1906 Geronimo (1829–1909), the revolutionary leader in the Apache War (1885–86) against the United States, dictates his memoirs

1910 With French chemist André Debierne (1874–1949), Marie isolates pure radium metal

1910-12 Soddy develops the concept of the isotope

1911 Marie wins the Nobel Prize for chemistry

1913 The Danish physicist Niels Bohr (1885–1962) proposes a model of the atom with orbiting electrons

1919 Rutherford announces the first artificial disintegration of an atom after changing nitrogen into oxygen and hydrogen

1920 Rutherford gives the name "proton" to positively charged subatomic particles, and predicts the discovery of an uncharged "neutron"

1925 French physicist Frédéric Joliot (1900–1958) becomes special assistant to Marie Currie. In 1926 he marries Irène Curie (1897–1956)

1932 The neutron is discovered by English physicist James Chadwick (1891–1974)

1934 Irène Joliot-Curie and Frédéric Joliot-Curie discover artificial radioactivity

After 1935

1938 Lise Meitner (1878–1968), Otto Frisch (1904–1979), and Otto Hahn (1879–1968) discover nuclear fission

1942 The first sustained nuclear reaction is produced by Italian physicist Enrico Fermi (1901–1954)

1910   **1915**   **1920**   **1925**   **1930**

1910 The Mexican Revolution begins, with the reformist leader Francisco Madero (1873–1913) opposing the dictator Porfirio Díaz (1830–1915)

1911 Russian-born American composer Irving Berlin (1888–1989) writes his first big ragtime hit, "Alexander's Ragtime Band." Over the next 30 years he will write songs for 19 Broadway shows and 18 films

1914 Serbian nationalist assassinates the heir to the Austrian throne; this marks the beginning of World War I (1914–18)

1917 The Bolshevik (Communist) Party seizes power in wartorn Russia

1917 In response to Germany's unrestricted submarine attacks, the United States enters World War I

1920 Women win the vote in the United States as the 19th Amendment to the Constitution is ratified

1920 In the United States the Westinghouse Company sets up the radio station KDKA; by 1922 there will be more than 500 radio stations in the United States

1922 Benito Mussolini (1883–1945) becomes fascist dictator of Italy; known as "Il Duce," he will ally Italy with Germany in 1936

1925 Joseph Stalin (1879–1953) takes power in the Soviet Union. He will dominate the Communist world for the next 28 years

1926 American professional baseball player George Herman "Babe" Ruth (1895–1948) hits 60 home runs in a major-league season, setting a record that will not be broken for 30 years

1929 In New York the Wall Street Crash ushers in the Great Depression, a collapse of world trade until the mid-1930s

ALBERT EINSTEIN

1879 –1955

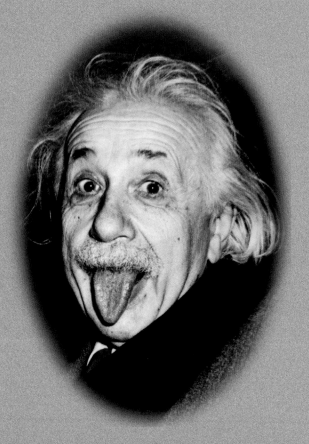

" Imagination is more important than knowledge. For knowledge is limited, whereas imagination embraces the entire world, stimulating progress, giving birth to evolution. It is...a real factor in scientific research. "

Albert Einstein

ALBERT EINSTEIN, THE BEST-KNOWN SCIENTIST OF THE 20TH CENTURY, PUBLISHED HIS SPECIAL THEORY OF RELATIVITY IN 1905, AND FOLLOWED THIS WITH HIS GENERAL THEORY OF RELATIVITY IN 1915. WIDELY BELIEVED TO BE THE GREATEST SCIENTIST SINCE THE ENGLISH MATHEMATICIAN, PHYSICIST, AND ASTRONOMER ISAAC NEWTON (1642-1727), EINSTEIN REVOLUTIONIZED OUR UNDERSTANDING OF THE UNIVERSE, AND HIS THEORIES LED TO THE DEVELOPMENT OF ATOMIC BOMBS AND NUCLEAR REACTORS.

Born in Ulm, Germany, on March14, 1879, Albert Einstein's childhood was unsettled. His father, Hermann Einstein, was a Jewish businessman whose commercial ventures meant that the family were always moving. In 1880 they went to Munich, and Hermann and his brother Jakob set up an electrical engineering business. But the enterprise did not fare well, and so the family left Germany for Italy. Albert, however, remained in Munich to finish his schooling. Although not a particularly gifted pupil, his uncles encouraged his interest in mathematics and science.

In 1896 he began studying at the Federal Polytechnic School in Zurich, Switzerland. Einstein had an independent approach to learning and read the works of great 19th-century physicists instead of attending lectures. Although he graduated in 1900, he failed to secure a university post, and instead became an examiner at the Bern Patent Office.

A MOMENTOUS YEAR

The year 1905 is best known as Einstein's "annus mirabilis," Latin for "wonder year." Einstein's accomplishment included fully worked-out theories, and five scientific papers, all of which were actually published in 1905, which was unusual because the theories and papers were not compiled by an academic, but by an unknown physicist working in an office.

PACKETS OF LIGHT

Scientists at the end of the 19th century believed that for light, electricity, and magnetic forces to travel through space, they must be carried in a medium known

Eminent scientists photographed in Brussels in 1927 at a conference on quantum theory. They include Max Planck, Marie Curie, Albert Einstein, and Werner Heisenberg.

as the ether. No one had been able to prove the existence of the ether, but there seemed to be no other explanation. Scottish physicist James Clerk Maxwell (1831–1879) had shown the connection between magnetism and electricity and demonstrated that electromagnetism was radiated in waves. Clerk Maxwell also showed that light is a form of electromagnetic wave.

One of Einstein's 1905 papers concerned the photoelectric effect, which is the way that some metals eject electrons when light shines on them. In 1899, the German physicist Philip Lenard (1862–1947) noted that when light fell on a metal surface, individual electrons were thrown off, and that their velocity seemed to be related to the color of the light.

KEY DATES

1879	March 14, born at Ulm, Germany
1896–1900	Studies at the Federal Polytechnic School, Zurich
1902	Begins work at the Swiss Patent Office, Bern
1905	Publishes special theory of relativity
1909	Appointed associate professor of physics at the University of Zurich
1911	Appointed professor at the University of Prague
1914–33	Serves as director of theoretical physics at the Kaiser Wilhelm Institute, Berlin
1915	Publishes general theory of relativity
1933	Leaves Germany for the United States
1955	April 18, dies in Princeton, New Jersey

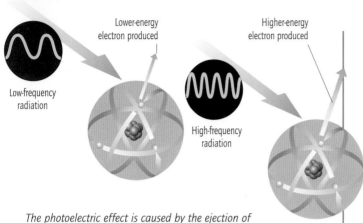

Lower-energy electron produced

Higher-energy electron produced

Low-frequency radiation

High-frequency radiation

The photoelectric effect is caused by the ejection of electrons from a sheet of metal in the path of a light beam. A quantum of low-frequency radiation (left) has less energy than one of high frequency (right). Einstein showed that the more energetic the light quanta (photons), the more energetic the electrons that are produced.

To explain this, Einstein adopted the idea of quanta that had been proposed by German physicist Max Planck (1858–1947) in 1900. Rather than traveling in waves, light could now be thought of as coming in tiny, separate packets, known as photons. Einstein assumed that every quantum of light would carry a

Hendrick Antoon Lorentz
1853-1928

As a professor of mathematical physics at Leiden University, Lorentz speculated that atoms of matter might be made up of charged particles, and that it is the movement of these that create light. He argued that a magnetic field would affect the movement of the particles, and therefore the wavelength of light. This was proved by his pupil, Pieter Zeeman (1865–1943), in 1896, and is known as the Zeeman Effect. For this discovery the pair were jointly awarded the Nobel Prize for physics in 1902. In 1904 Lorentz developed the idea that moving objects approaching the speed of light contract in the direction of motion, as also predicted by Einstein's special theory of relativity.

specific amount of energy related to the light's frequency. The frequency of light is what determines its color. Blue light has a higher frequency than red and would therefore strike the metal's surface more energetically than red light, and would cause more energetic photons to be emitted. Because all light quanta of the same color have the same frequency and therefore the same energy, increasing the amount of light falling on the metal's surface will not produce more energetic electrons; it will simply produce more quanta to throw off more electrons.

Photons and quanta are more familiar concepts to us today, but they were treated with very deep suspicion by Einstein's colleagues in 1905. It was only when, in 1916, the processes described by Einstein were experimentally confirmed by American physicist Robert Millikan (1868–1953), that Einstein's views gained wide acceptance. It was for this work that Einstein was awarded the 1921 Nobel Prize for physics.

SPECIAL THEORY OF RELATIVITY

Einstein developed his ideas to imagine what it would be like to travel as fast as light. He wrote about them in another of his 1905 papers, *On the Electrodynamics of Moving Bodies*, in which he developed what is now known as his special theory of relativity.

The theory concerns movement or motion, and the term "special" arises because it deals with only one special kind of motion, namely what is called uniform motion. This is motion in a straight line at a constant speed. We can look out of a train window and see that we are moving by watching the trees flash by. But this is relative motion, and demonstrates only that we are moving relative to the trees, or that the trees are moving relative to the train. If there were no windows and the train moved smoothly at a constant speed, there would be nothing we could do to find out whether we were at rest or in uniform motion. Einstein named this the principle of relativity.

Einstein added as a second principle that the speed of light is constant. This had already been established by James Clerk Maxwell, but because it went against common sense, scientists had tended to dismiss it.

RELATIVE TIME

Observer A is in the middle of a train, which is moving at a uniform speed. Two bolts of lightning strike the ground at C and D, equidistant from A. Observer B, who is standing at the side of the track directly opposite A, sees both bolts hit the ground at the same time. But observer A, who is moving toward D, will see D before C because the light from D will have a shorter distance to travel to A. Thus for A, events C and D do not happen at the same time.

It follows also that time cannot run at the same rate for two observers if one is moving. Imagine two observers, X and Y, are sitting facing each other in a train (see right). X shines a flashlight and the light travels in a straight line to observer Y. A third stationary observer, Z, at the side of the track, watches the train go by. But as the light from the flashlight travels from X to Y the train will have moved on and Z will see light travel from X to Y" (said "Y prime"). But the path X–Y is shorter than the path X–Y". The speed of light is the same for all observers. So if while light travels from X to Y, the observer Z sees the same light travel from X to Y", and the path X–Y is shorter than X–Y", then time must pass more quickly for observer Z.

The argument that there is no "absolute" time is the source of the "twins paradox." One 21-year-old twin stays on Earth while the other goes off in a spaceship. Say the spaceship travels at 95 percent of the speed of light for 15 years. The nearer the speed of light an object travels, the more its length decreases, and its mass increases. An effect of this would be that time measured on a clock on board would pass more slowly; in the time it took to record 20 minutes on an Earth-based clock, the spaceship clock would record one hour. So while 15 years pass on Earth, only five years go by on the spaceship. On return to Earth the astronaut would be 26 years old (21 + 5) but his twin would be aged 36 (21 + 15).

In his special theory of relativity Einstein argued that time is relative (below), and that, because the speed of light is the same for all observers, time can run at different rates for different people (right).

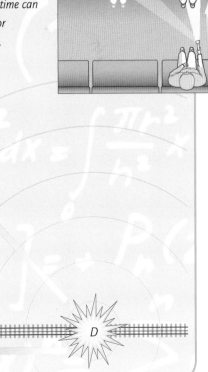

B

A

C

D

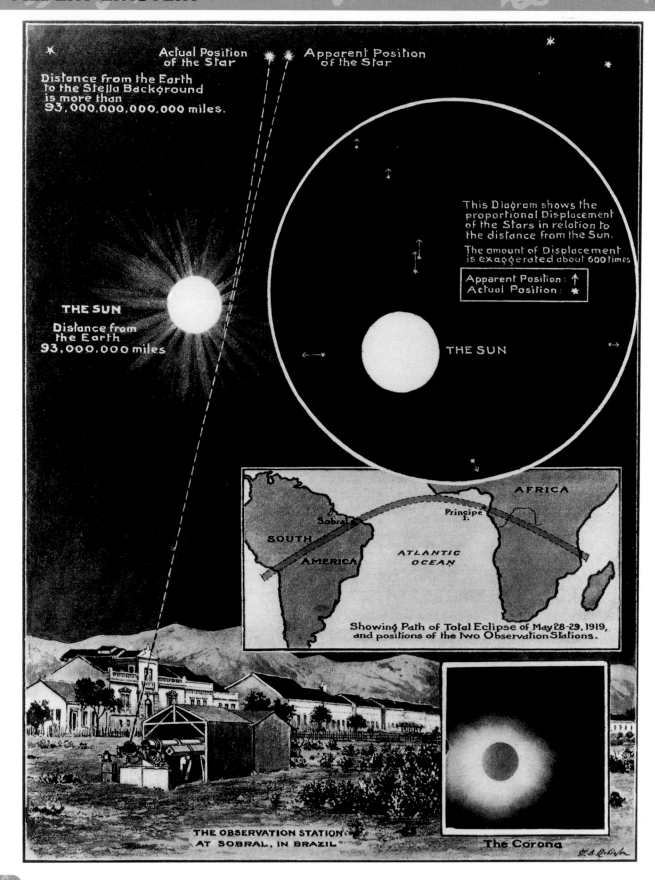

Actual Position of the Star

Apparent Position of the Star

Distance from the Earth to the Stella Background is more than 93,000,000,000,000 miles.

THE SUN

Distance from the Earth 93,000,000 miles

This Diagram shows the proportional Displacement of the Stars in relation to the distance from the Sun.

The amount of Displacement is exaggerated about 600 times

Apparent Position : ↑
Actual Position : ✳

THE SUN

AFRICA

Principe I.

Sobral

SOUTH AMERICA

ATLANTIC OCEAN

Showing Path of Total Eclipse of May 28-29, 1919, and positions of the two Observation Stations.

THE OBSERVATION STATION AT SOBRAL, IN BRAZIL

The Corona

After all, reason seems to suggest that if we are traveling along and shine a flashlight in the direction we are moving, the light will travel at our speed plus the speed of light. If we shine the light in the opposite direction, we expect it to travel at the speed of light minus our speed. Einstein insisted that this is not so: the speed in both cases is the same; it is the speed of light.

Einstein also stated that nothing can move faster than the speed of light, 186,000 miles per second (299,274 km per second). But according to Newton's laws of motion, a force applied to an object causes acceleration, so in theory it would be possible to accelerate an object indefinitely until it was traveling faster than the speed of light. However, an object's acceleration depends on its mass. The less its mass, the greater its acceleration. Einstein suggested that a force applied to an object provides not only acceleration but also an increase in mass. As the accelerated body approaches the speed of light, its mass increases so dramatically that it would require an infinite force to accelerate it beyond this point.

AN EQUATION TO CHANGE THE WORLD

In another of his 1905 papers, Einstein set out one of the most famous formulas in physics, $E = mc^2$. This means that energy (E) equals mass (m) times the square of the speed of light (c). Physicists knew that certain elements emit a flow of energy called radiation when they break down. In 1938 German chemist Otto Hahn (1879–1968) bombarded uranium with neutrons. Hahn found that the uranium split into several products including the lighter element barium. But the total mass of the barium and everything else that formed was slightly less than that of the original uranium. The "missing" mass had been converted into energy in accordance with Einstein's formula. The amount of energy liberated was tiny. But scientists knew that a

Einstein challenged the longheld view that light always travels in a straight line. Instead, he theorized that a large object such as the Sun might exert such a strong gravitational pull that light rays close to it would bend. This theory, illustrated (opposite) in a newspaper, was proved correct during the 1919 eclipse.

RELATIVITY THEORY

To understand Einstein's general theory, imagine space as a rubbery sheet. A heavy object like the Sun (A) would make a dip in the sheet. This dip represents its gravitational pull. Rather than seeing the gravitational pull as being present in the body of the Sun, as Newton had, Einstein saw it in the space around it (which is not closed as shown here). Any slow-moving body traveling nearby (such as Earth or another planet) would "roll" into the dip created by (A) and follow a path (B) within it. Faster-moving bodies would follow a more open curve around A, while a ray of light (C), which is much farther away and traveling much faster, would only curve slightly.

single gram of uranium contains more than 2.5×10^{22} atoms. It was clear that just one gram of uranium had the potential to release staggering amounts of energy.

GENERAL THEORY OF RELATIVITY

In his general theory (1915), Einstein considered acceleration. Its central idea, known as the "equivalence principle," states that the inertial mass and gravitational mass of an object are the same. Mass can be defined in two ways. Inertial mass is a measure of the extent to which a body resists acceleration when a force is applied to it. The more massive an object is, the

ALBERT EINSTEIN

Such was Einstein's fame throughout the world that his portrait, and even his famous equation, adorned postage stamps and banknotes from Ghana in West Africa to Israel.

greater is the force needed to accelerate it. Gravitational mass is produced by gravity, the attractive force between any planet and a body in its gravitational field.

According to Einstein's general theory, the curvature of space can be seen as distortions in space produced by the presence of massive bodies such as the Sun. A planet moving at the right speed and in the right direction as it approaches the Sun would be caught in the dip produced by the Sun's gravitational pull, and then continue to move around it in a curved path. Because the distortion is less pronounced at greater distances from the Sun, distant objects are attracted less.

A 1930s cartoon has Russian-born American physicist George Gamow (1904–1968) playing billiards with quantum balls. The caption—"The white ball went in all directions"— acknowledges that science no longer consisted of certainties.

THE ECLIPSE OF 1919

A total eclipse of the Sun was forecast for 1919, an event that was immediately seen by physicists as a crucial test of the general theory.

Because the Sun is the object with the strongest gravitational field in the Solar System, light passing close to the Sun should be

EINSTEIN THE PACIFIST

Einstein had what he termed "a passionate sense of social justice and social responsibility" that stayed with him throughout his life. He was a pacifist and, after his move to Berlin in 1914, he spoke out against Germany's strong military build-up. But nothing could prevent the inevitable march toward war in Europe. By August that year, World War I had begun.

Einstein continued to promote his pacifist views within wartorn Germany. He felt that the whole world was undergoing an "epidemic delusion" that later generations would not understand. However, when the war ended in 1918, Einstein genuinely believed that Germany had renounced militarism, and that the setting up of the League of Nations to promote peace and international security in 1919 would halt any further aggression.

The New Jewish State

Although Einstein was Jewish, he had not been brought up in a religious home. However, he always insisted that "I am a Jew, and I am glad to belong to the Jewish people." A growth in anti-Semitism in Berlin after World War I led to his being attacked for his "communist" views, and this worsened when he declared himself a Zionist, a member of the political movement supporting the rights of the Jewish people to establish a national home in Palestine (this aim was achieved in 1948 with the founding of Israel). In 1921 Einstein went with Russian-born chemist and statesman Chaim Weizmann (1874–1952), later first president of Israel, on a fundraising tour of the United States.

deflected from its straight-line path, but the Sun emits so much of its own light that any other rays that pass close to it go by unobserved. However, during a total eclipse the Sun's light is blocked out for a few minutes by the Moon, and for that time other stars are visible during the day. Einstein predicted that the gravitational

On the death of Weizmann in 1952, Einstein was invited to become the new president of Israel, but he declined, claiming that he lacked "the natural aptitude and the experience."

War and Peace

The 1932 World Disarmament Conference in Geneva was intended to persuade countries to get rid of their weapons. Einstein committed time and great effort to its success, and was distressed when talks broke down. In the following year Nazi leader Adolf Hitler (1889–1945) became chancellor of Germany, and the persecution of Jewish citizens began. Einstein left Germany and moved to the United States. In 1939 he wrote a famous letter to President Roosevelt warning of the atomic threat. After the atom bomb was dropped on Hiroshima, Japan, in August 1945, Einstein headed the campaign by scientists protesting its use.

The burning of "un-German" books (above) in the time of the Nazis. Einstein's 1939 letter (below) warned Roosevelt of the atomic threat.

pull of the Sun would deflect the light of a star by a precise amount, and the star itself would seem to change its position. He also predicted that stars in the same direction of the sky as the Sun, but much farther away, would not change their position because they were unaffected by the Sun's gravity.

The eclipse was observed from Sobral in Brazil and from the island of Príncipe, off West Africa, from where it was reported that "the results...gave a definite displacement in good accordance with Einstein's theory." News that Einstein's predictions had been confirmed made headlines around the world.

ALBERT EINSTEIN

SCIENTIFIC BACKGROUND

Before 1905

The British physicist James Clerk Maxwell (1831–1879) proposes that light travels in electromagnetic waves

The Dutch physicists Hendrick Lorenz (1853–1928) and Pieter Zeeman (1865–1943) establish that an intense magnetic field affects the wavelengths of light

The American physicists Albert Michelson (1852–1931) and Edward Morley (1838–1923) discover that the speed of light is constant

The German physicist Max Planck (1858–1947) introduces the theory that energy consists of indivisible units (quanta)

1905 Albert Einstein publishes papers on his special theory of relativity, the photoelectric effect, Brownian motion, and the "Equivalence Principle" (that energy is related to mass by the equation $E = mc^2$)

1909 Einstein calls for a theory that will reconcile the fact that light sometimes acts as a wave and sometimes as a particle

1909 Lithuanian mathematician Hermann Minkowski (1864–1909) proposes a four-dimensional model in which space and time are inseparable, paving the way for Einstein's general theory of relativity

1911 Einstein makes the prediction (later to be incorporated into his general theory of relativity) that light passing near the Sun will be found to be deflected by the Sun's gravity

1913 The Danish physicist Niels Bohr (1885–1962) proposes a model of the atom in which electrons are arranged in rings around its nucleus

1915 Einstein publishes his general theory of relativity, concerning accelerated motion. One of its predictions is that a red shift will occur if light passes through an intense gravitational field

1919 Einstein's prediction that the gravitational pull of the Sun can bend light is confirmed during a solar eclipse

---

1905 **1910** **1915**

POLITICAL AND CULTURAL BACKGROUND

1906 Britain launches the battleship *Dreadnought*, part of an intense naval arms race with Germany and other European powers

1909 The *Jungendherberge* (Youth Hostel) movement is founded in Germany for students on walking tours

1913 The Keystone Picture Corporation signs up British comedian Charlie Chaplin (1889–1977), who will make 35 films in his first year

1914 World War I (1914–18) breaks out in Europe; after rapid advances through Belgium and northern France in August, German forces are halted at the Battle of the Marne, north of Paris

1916 In France, the Germans and French each lose 400,000 dead or wounded in the Battle of Verdun

1918 Summer advances in France exhaust the Germany army, which collapses in the fall. By November World War I is over

1921 Einstein wins the Nobel Prize for Physics for his work on the photoelectric effect

1922 Einstein's first paper on Unified Field Theory—which is his attempt to explain electric, magnetic, and gravitational forces in terms of each other—is not successful

1923 Einstein supports work published by the French physicist Louis-Victor de Broglie (1892–1987) showing how subatomic particles can be regarded as waves

1925 The gravitational red-shift predicted by Einstein is confirmed in astronomical observations

1926 Inspired by de Broglie's work, the Austrian physicist Erwin Schrödinger (1887–1961) introduces wave mechanics

1927 Werner Heisenberg (1901–1976) proposes his Uncertainty Principle: we can never know simultaneously the position and momentum of a subatomic particle

1929 American astronomer Edwin Hubble (1889–1953) establishes that the universe is expanding

1930 Einstein expresses support for the Dutch astronomer Willem de Sitter (1872–1934), who argues that Einstein's general theory of relativity, applied to the universe, favors the idea of an expanding universe

1935 Einstein publishes a paper critical of quantum theory

1938 The German physicist Otto Hahn (1879–1968) splits the uranium atom

1942 Italian physicist Enrico Fermi (1901–1954) achieves the first sustained nuclear chain reaction

After 1945

1953 Einstein presents his final paper, on Unified Field Theory

1965 German-born American astrophysicist Arno Penzias (1933–) and American radioastronomer Robert Wilson (1936–) discover cosmic microwave background radiation, which supports the "hot big bang" theory of the origin of the universe

---

1920 | **1925** | **1930** | **1935** | **1940**

1920 In the United States wartime alcohol restrictions are extended to a complete ban on drinking: Prohibition lasts for 13 years

1921 Einstein takes part in a fund-raising tour of the United States in support of Zionism (the establishment of a Jewish homeland)

1925 In Germany, Adolf Hitler (1889–1945) publishes Volume 1 of *Mein Kampf* (My Struggle), his plan to make Germany great by warring against Jews and Communists

1929 Chicago's Mafia gang warfare over control of bootlegging (smuggling) liquor reaches its height with the St. Valentine's Day Massacre, in which seven are killed

1933 With Adolf Hitler about to take power in Germany, Einstein emigrates to the United States; more than 150,000 other Jews will emigrate from Germany

1935 Overcultivation and drought over vast areas of the United States' Great Plains leads to huge dust storms; up to 350,000 people are forced to leave the "Dust Bowl" in search of new homes and work

1936 American author Margaret Mitchell (1900–1949) publishes *Gone with the Wind*, which sells a million copies in six months

1937 American artist and film director Walt Disney completes his first full-length feature film, Snow White and the Seven Dwarfs

1941 The United States enters World War II (1939–45) after Japanese planes attack the U.S. Navy base at Pearl Harbor

NIELS BOHR AND WERNER HEISENBERG

1885-1962 and 1901-1976

"In science...it is impossible to open up new territory unless one is prepared to leave the safe anchorage of established doctrine and run the risk of a hazardous leap forward...."

Werner Heisenberg
Physics and Beyond (1971)

NIELS BOHR WAS A DANISH PHYSICIST WHO PRODUCED A MODEL OF ATOMIC STRUCTURE THAT SOLVED MANY OF THE PUZZLES ABOUT HOW RADIATION OCCURS. THE GERMAN PHYSICIST WERNER HEISENBERG WAS A PIONEER IN THE DEVELOPMENT OF QUANTUM MECHANICS, WHICH EXPLAINS HOW ELECTRONS AND NUCLEI BEHAVE. HOWEVER, EVENTS IN EUROPE FOLLOWING HITLER'S ASCENT AND THE START OF WORLD WAR II DISRUPTED THE CAREERS OF BOTH OF THESE SCIENTISTS.

Niels Bohr's father, Christian (1855-1911), was a professor of physiology at Copenhagen University, Denmark, and his younger brother Harald (1887-1951) was an eminent mathematician. Niels Bohr's son, Aage (1922-), shared the Nobel Prize for physics in 1975 for his work on the shape of atomic nuclei. Bohr was awarded a doctorate from Copenhagen University in 1911 for a paper on the behavior of electrons in metals. That same year he joined the research team at the University of Manchester, England, headed by physicist Ernest Rutherford (1871-1937), that was studying the structure of the atom.

BUILDING AN ATOMIC MODEL

The word atom is from the Greek meaning, "that which cannot be divided," and when English scientist John Dalton (1766-1844) devised his theory of the atom in the 19th century, he saw it as a tiny, solid particle. By the beginning of the 20th century a new picture of the atom was emerging. Rutherford showed that it had a heavy, positively charged nucleus, around which much lighter, negatively charged electrons orbited. Rutherford pictured electrons moving in much the same way that the planets orbit the Sun in our universe, so his model became known as the "planetary" model of the atom.

There was a difference between atoms and planets, however. The force that keeps the planets orbiting the Sun is gravity, but the electrons orbiting an atomic nucleus are electrically charged. According to the rules of physics, accelerating electrically charged particles give off energy, causing them to slow down. This loss of energy should cause orbiting electrons to collapse extremely rapidly into the central nucleus of the atom.

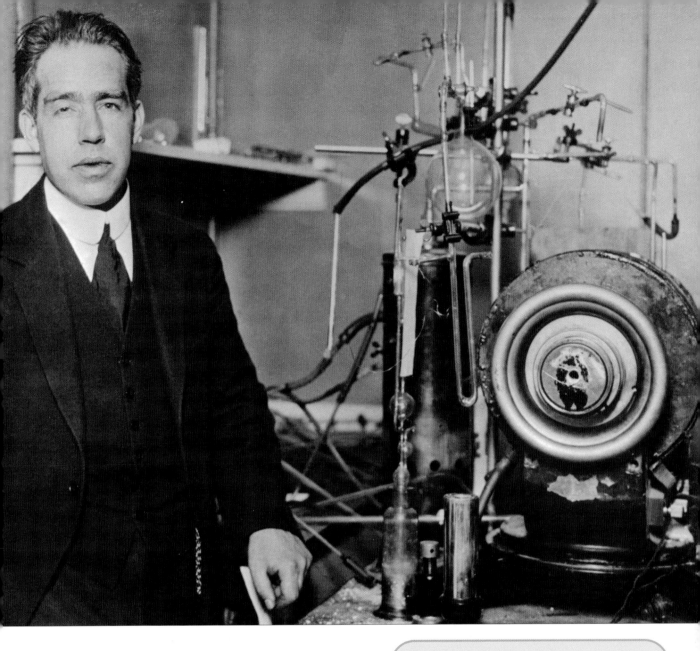

Niels Bohr in his laboratory at the Institute of Theoretical Physics in Copenhagen, which he founded in 1918.

This was obviously not happening, and it led some people to question the accuracy of Rutherford's model.

Bohr turned to the description of light offered by German physicist Max Planck (1858–1947) in 1900 to see if it would explain the behavior of electrons. Planck had stated that light is emitted in separate packets or "quanta," also known as photons. This was the beginning of "quantum theory," which revolutionized physics early in the 20th century. Planck found that the energy of the photons equals their frequency multiplied by a very tiny number known as Planck's constant (h).

KEY DATES

1911	Bohr begins working with Rutherford at Manchester University, England
1913	Bohr proposes new model for the atom
1922	Bohr is awarded Nobel Prize for physics
1924–26	Heisenberg works with Bohr in Copenhagen
1927	Heisenberg proposes his uncertainty principle
1932	Heisenberg is awarded Nobel Prize for physics
1939–45	Heisenberg directs German atomic bomb program
1943	Bohr flees occupied Denmark

Using Planck's quantum theory as a basis for his work, Bohr declared that in certain orbits electrons are stable: they neither lose nor gain energy as they move. The momentum (mass multiplied by speed) of an electron in a stable orbit is always a whole-number multiple of Planck's constant h: $1h$, $2h$, $3h$, and so on. According to Bohr's atomic model, the orbiting electrons are limited to a series of possible orbits. Energy is radiated or absorbed—lost or gained—only when electrons jump either to a higher-energy orbit or to a lower one. When an electron moves from a higher to a lower-energy state, it emits a photon of energy equal to the difference between the energies of the two states. When an electron moves from a lower to a higher state it absorbs a photon, which has the same energy as the difference between the energies of the two states.

Bohr's argument, described in his 1913 paper *On the Constitution of Atoms and Molecules*, showed why Rutherford's model of the atom was basically correct, and provided scientists with a convincing explanation as to why the atom was stable rather than unstable.

THE COLORS OF HYDROGEN

When elements are heated, they give off light that covers a specific range of frequencies or wavelengths and is therefore of a particular color. This is known as a

spectrum, and it enables elements to be identified by the light they emit. So, for example, the yellow light given off by sodium street lights is the specific set of frequencies of the element sodium. Bohr's 1913 account of the atom was tested against—and partly inspired by—the spectrum of the hydrogen atom. When hydrogen is heated and its light is passed through a prism—a transparent triangular solid used to refract light—its spectrum consists of a series of colored lines (known as spectral lines). Each line represents light of a particular wavelength. Bohr realized that the lines in the hydrogen spectrum were caused by electrons jumping between higher-energy and lower-energy orbits. When the electrons jump they emit a photon of light of a particular frequency, which appears as a line. All gases, when heated, produce spectral lines.

This diagram of an atom shows how electrons orbit the nucleus. Atoms absorb or emit light in packets known as photons. When electrons absorb photons they move to an orbit farther away from the nucleus, and when electrons emit photons they move to an orbit nearer to the nucleus.

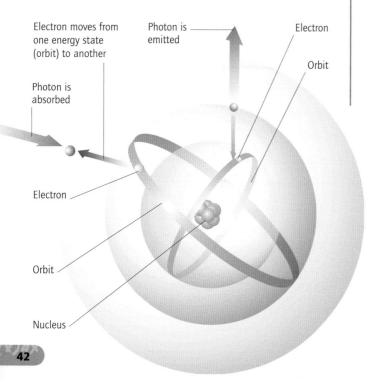

Electron moves from one energy state (orbit) to another

Photon is emitted

Electron

Orbit

Photon is absorbed

Electron

Orbit

Nucleus

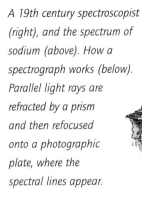

Spectroscopists examine the spectrum of light from a star which is captured on film; from it they can work out its chemical makeup. It is possible with spectroscopy to study atomic and molecular structures.

A 19th century spectroscopist (right), and the spectrum of sodium (above). How a spectrograph works (below). Parallel light rays are refracted by a prism and then refocused onto a photographic plate, where the spectral lines appear.

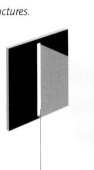
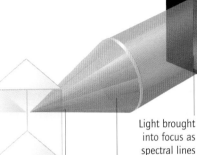

Light enters through entrance slit

Special "collimator" lens forms light into parallel rays

Prism refracts light

Camera lens

Light brought into focus as spectral lines

Photographic plate

FLEEING FROM WAR

In 1918 Bohr headed a new Institute of Theoretical Physics in Copenhagen, and in 1922 he was awarded the Nobel Prize in physics for his work on atomic theory. During the next 20 years the Institute became the world center for the new quantum physics, attracting scientists from many countries. Bohr lectured extensively in Europe, Canada, and the United States.

In April 1940, German troops occupied Denmark. Bohr, who was Jewish, did not conceal his anti-Nazi views. He struggled to keep the Institute going, but in September 1943 he was warned that he was about to be arrested by the Nazis and fled to Sweden. By December Bohr was in the United States working on the Manhattan atom bomb project at Los Alamos. But he was increasingly concerned about the dangers of nuclear weapons and was convinced that the best way of controlling them was by the free exchange of

knowledge between scientists and governments. After the war, he campaigned for the peaceful use of nuclear energy and cofounded the European Center for Nuclear Research (CERN). He died in Copenhagen in 1962.

A MATHEMATICAL SOLUTION TO THE ATOM

Werner Heisenberg was born in Würzburg, Germany. He studied physics at the University of Munich and Göttingen University and gained a doctorate in 1923.

Then he traveled to Copenhagen and worked for two years with Bohr at the Institute for Theoretical Physics. In 1927 he became professor of theoretical physics at the University of Leipzig in Germany.

Faced with the many conflicting ideas that were emerging about quantum theory, Heisenberg determined to construct a

German troops in Ålborg, Denmark, in April 1940. Germany's occupation of Denmark brought a quick halt to Bohr's dream of the Institute as a center of international research and cooperation.

43

Louis-Victor de Broglie
1892–1987

Louis-Victor de Broglie was born in Dieppe in northern France. He originally studied as a historian, but his brother was a physicist who pioneered the study of X-rays, and he stimulated Louis-Victor's interest in science. After serving in the army during World War I (1914–18), Louis-Victor returned to the Sorbonne University in Paris to study physics, gaining his doctorate in the subject in 1924.

Einstein and others had already proposed that waves (of light, for example) can behave like particles. De Broglie put forward the converse idea: that particles, particularly electrons, can behave as waves. The associated wavelength, he calculated, equals Planck's constant (h) divided by the momentum of the electron. His theory was proved to be correct in 1927 when British physicist George Thomson (1892–1975) made a stream of electrons pass through a thin gold foil and produce diffraction patterns on a photographic plate. Diffraction is a property of wave motion that occurs when a wave is deflected by an obstacle in its path. When light waves pass through a narrow slit and fall upon a screen, diffraction is seen as a pattern of alternating light and dark bands.

Also in 1927, American physicist Clinton Davisson (1881–1958) made a finding similar to Thomson's by directing an angled electron beam onto a nickel surface. De Broglie was awarded the 1929 Nobel Prize for physics for discovering the wave nature of the electron, and in 1937 Davisson and Thomson received the same prize for their experimental work in proving it.

What could be observed about the hydrogen atom was its spectrum. Heisenberg began to write down the differences between the observed frequencies in the hydrogen spectrum and arranged them as a set of figures in a square pattern (see below).

Heisenberg was able to construct equations that gave the frequencies and other observed properties of the spectral lines, but he ran into a serious problem. We know that if we add or multiply two numbers, the order in which we add or multiply the numbers does not matter. For example, 7 x 8 = 56, as does 8 x 7. Mathematicians say that such operations "commute," or are "commutative." But Heisenberg found that some of his quantum states did not commute: that p x q, for example, did not equal q x p.

A solution was provided by Max Born (1882–1970), then professor of physics at Göttingen University. He drew Heisenberg's attention to a branch of mathematics known as matrix mathematics. A matrix is the mathematical term for arrays of numbers set out in rows and columns, just like Heisenberg's frequencies. As Heisenberg had discovered, the multiplication of matrices is not commutative. Heisenberg reworked his early calculations, presenting the results in 1925.

THE DEVELOPMENT OF QUANTUM MECHANICS

Using this system, it was possible to find a mathematical explanation of atomic structure. Heisenberg's model was fundamental to the development of quantum mechanics, the laws determining the behavior of small-scale physical phenomena such as electrons

Atomic structure can be calculated mathematically with Heisenberg's matrix. Here S stands for electron states, or orbits; V stands for frequency. So, for example, if the electron in an atom jumps from S_1 to S_4, we can see from the table that the frequency of the photon emitted will be V_4-1.

	S_1	S_2	S_3	S_4
S_1	V_1-1	V_2-1	V_3-1	V_4-1
S_2	V_1-2	V_2-2	V_3-2	V_4-2
S_3	V_1-3	V_2-3	V_3-3	V_4-3
S_4	V_1-4	V_2-4	V_3-4	V_4-4

mathematical system that would explain the structure of the atom. He believed it was a mistake to think of the atom in visual terms, like the planetary model that Rutherford had described. Heisenberg only wanted to deal with what could be established by experiment.

and nuclei. Pauli's exclusion theory (1925), developed by Wolfgang Pauli (1900–1958), was an important factor. It asserts that no two electrons in an atom can be in the same state or configuration at the same time.

Erwin Schrödinger (1887–1961), meanwhile, was formulating a theory to describe the behavior of electrons in atoms based on de Broglie's proposal that particles in some situations act like waves (see box opposite). He described a "wave equation" with which he was able to predict broadly where, at any given point, the electron in the hydrogen atom might be found in relation to its nucleus. This approach to quantum mechanics became known as wave mechanics. For most people, envisaging particles as waves was much easier than struggling with Heisenberg's matrices, and Schrödinger's wave theory gained more general acceptance. Nevertheless the value of Heisenberg's matrix mechanics was recognized with the award of the 1932 Nobel Prize for physics. Schrödinger shared it the following year with English theoretical physicist Paul Dirac (1902–1984). It was Dirac who showed that wave and matrix mechanics lead to the same answers.

HEISENBERG'S UNCERTAINTY PRINCIPLE

Heisenberg is firmly linked with the "uncertainty principle," which he formulated in 1927. An alternative description for it is the "indeterminacy principle." Heisenberg's principle states that the position and the momentum of an object cannot both be measured at exactly the same time, even in theory. It is not something we notice in everyday life—it is obviously possible to know simultaneously the position and the velocity of an automobile, for example. This is because

the uncertainties implied by the principle are far too small to be observed in ordinary objects. Only on the level of minute subatomic particles such as electrons, neutrons, or photons does the principle become significant. It is possible to know the position of an electron, or to know its momentum, but not both at the same time. People often think that the "uncertainty" arises because instruments simply cannot measure position and momentum at the same time, but the uncertainty principle in fact reflects the dual particle–wave nature of particles.

Heisenberg's uncertainty principle disturbed many scientists, including Albert Einstein (1879–1955). It has been fiercely debated and analyzed ever since, yet the uncertainty principle has survived its critics and remains today one of the fundamental planks of quantum mechanics.

THE EFFECTS OF WAR

In 1933 the Nazi leader Adolf Hitler (1889–1945) assumed power in Germany. Almost immediately the purge of Jewish scientists from universities and laboratories began. Many other scientists left Germany during the 1930s in protest, but Heisenberg chose to remain. Like Max Planck (then in his late seventies), who also stayed in Germany, Heisenberg was anxious to try to protect German scientific traditions and institutions. Although he was hostile to the policies of the Nazi regime, he did

Erwin Schrödinger succeeded Planck as professor of physics at the University of Berlin, but left Germany when the Nazis took over.

NIELS BOHR AND WERNER HEISENBERG

not openly oppose them. In 1941 Heisenberg took up a post as director of Kaiser Wilhelm Institute for Physics in Berlin.

After the war, Heisenberg returned to Göttingen. He wanted to restore the reputation of German science in the world and to revive research in his country. He founded and directed the Max Planck Institute for Physics for research in astrophysics and theoretical physics, which moved to Munich in 1948. After the defeat of Germany in 1945, the occupying Allies banned German scientists from researching into nuclear fission. Heisenberg tried to overturn this ban, arguing that the technology should be restricted to the production of nuclear energy, not nuclear weaponry. When, partly through the efforts of Niels Bohr, the European Council for Nuclear Research

Delegates at a conference at the Institute for Theoretical Physics in Copenhagen in 1930. Bohr and Heisenberg are second and third from left in the front row; on Heisenberg's right is Wolfgang Pauli. Pauli and Heisenberg were students together at the University of Munich, and they remained lifelong friends.

(CERN) was established in 1952, Heisenberg headed its scientific policy committee. He also continued his work on quantum theory and elementary particles until he retired in 1970. In 1953 he became the first president of the Alexander von Humboldt Foundation, Bonn. He died in Munich on February 1, 1976.

WAS A NAZI ATOMIC BOMB A POSSIBILITY?

In 1938 German scientists Otto Hahn and Lise Meitner (1878–1968) split the nuclei of uranium atoms; this is called nuclear fission. Nuclear fission releases massive amounts of energy, and it was clear it might be used to create weapons of enormous power. Niels Bohr brought news of what Hahn and Meitner had done when he visited the United States in January 1939. With the outbreak of World War II, fears that Germany might be the first to exploit nuclear fission grew more acute. Bohr's warning helped fuel the concern that led the U.S. government to set up the Manhattan Project. Meanwhile Heisenberg, in Germany, was ordered by the Army Weapons Office to see if an atomic bomb could be made.

A Mystery Visit

In 1941 Heisenberg called on Niels Bohr in Copenhagen. There has been much controversy about why he made this visit. Bohr had been Heisenberg's mentor in the 1920s, but since April 1940 Denmark had been occupied by Germany. Heisenberg was now a representative of a conquering power. Some think Heisenberg wanted to find

out how close the United States was to developing nuclear weapons; others say he came to warn Bohr about German progress. Heisenberg himself later claimed that he would have sabotaged attempts by German scientists to create an atomic bomb, and that he was suggesting that Bohr should do the same on the Allied side.

The Farm Hall Tapes

In 1945 Heisenberg and other German scientists were captured by the Allies and taken to Farm Hall, near Cambridge, England. The group's conversations were secretly taped, including their reaction to news that the Americans had dropped an atomic bomb on Hiroshima in Japan on August 6, 1945. The tapes seem to confirm that German scientists never really knew how to develop a fission weapon; Heisenberg is heard to exclaim, "I don't believe a word about the bomb." As the Manhattan Project showed, nothing less than an all-out program using every available resource was needed to produce a viable atomic weapon. It now seems clear that in war-pressed Germany these resources were simply not available.

Before 1910

English scientist John Dalton (1766–1844) devises his theory of the atom as a tiny solid particle

German physicist Max Planck (1858–1947) suggests that light is emitted in separate packets called "quanta," or photons

1911 British physicist Ernest Rutherford (1871–1937) discovers that atoms have nuclei

1913 Bohr proposes a new model of the atom

1922 Bohr is awarded the Nobel Prize for physics

1924 French physicist Louis-Victor de Broglie (1892–1987) establishes the wave nature of electrons

1927 Heisenberg proposes his uncertainty principle

1932 Heisenberg is awarded the Nobel Prize for physics

1932 English physicist James Chadwick (1891–1974) discovers the neutron

1940 German-born scientists Otto Frisch (1904–1979) and Rudolf Peierls (1907–1995) calculate that it would only take a pound or two of uranium 235 to build an atomic bomb

1943 Bohr begins work on the Manhattan Project at Los Alamos, New Mexico

1952 Heisenberg becomes head of the scientific policy committee of the European Council for Nuclear Research (CERN)

1962 Bohr dies on November 18

1964 American theoretical physicist Murray Gell-Mann (1929–) proposes that quarks are the fundamental building blocks of matter

1965 American physicists Richard Feynman (1918–1988) and Julian Schwinger (1918–1994), and Japanese physicist Sin-Itiro Tomonaga (1906–1979), receive the Nobel Prize for physics for their work on quantum electrodynamics

1976 Heisenberg dies on February 2

1986 Individual quantum jumps in individual atoms are observed

After 1990

1995 Particle physicists in Illinois identify the last of the six "flavors" of quarks, the elementary particles predicted by Gell-Mann in 1964; the six are known as: up, down, strange, charmed, bottom, and top

---

1910   **1930**   **1950**   **1970**

1915 A secret treaty between the Allies and Italy brings Italy into World War I (1914–18) on the Allied side

1922 The first issue of the monthly magazine *Reader's Digest* is published in the United States; it will become the world's biggest-selling magazine

1933 In Germany the Nazis launch a campaign of persecution against the Jews, closing down Jewish-owned shops and ousting Jewish professors from universities

1939 The invasion of Poland by Germany on September 1 marks the beginning of World War II (1939–45)

1943 *Casablanca*, a wartime romance starring Humphrey Bogart (1899–1957) and Ingrid Bergman (1915–1982), wins the Academy Award for best motion picture

1950 Vietnam is effectively split in two after Britain and the United States recognize the emperor Bao Dai (1913–1997) as its ruler—one week after the Soviet Union and its allies endorsed the regime led by communist Ho Chi Minh (1892–1969) in the north

1962 The Cuban missile crisis erupts as the United States blockades Cuba to prevent the installation of Soviet missiles there

1976 *All the President's Men*, a film starring Dustin Hoffman (1937–) and Robert Redford (1937–), dramatizes the events surrounding the 1972 Watergate scandal

1978 In the United States President Jimmy Carter (1924–) hosts talks between the leaders of Egypt and Israel at Camp David; a framework treaty is signed, ending 30 years of hostility between the two countries

JULIUS ROBERT OPPENHEIMER

1904-1967

" There must be no barriers to freedom of inquiry. There is no place for dogma in science. The scientist is free, and must be free to ask any question, to doubt any assertion, to seek for any evidence, to correct any error."

J. Robert Oppenheimer
The Open Mind (1955)

IN 1943 AMERICAN NUCLEAR PHYSICIST JULIUS ROBERT OPPENHEIMER BECAME DIRECTOR OF THE MANHATTAN PROJECT—THE U.S. GOVERNMENT RESEARCH PROGRAM FOR DEVELOPING THE ATOMIC BOMB. OPPENHEIMER'S OPPOSITION TO THE MAKING OF THE MUCH MORE POWERFUL HYDROGEN BOMB, AND HIS PAST COMMUNIST LINKS, CAUSED HIM TO BE INVESTIGATED BY A MILITARY SECURITY COMMITTEE IN 1953.

B orn into a wealthy New York family, from 1922 Oppenheimer attended Harvard University and then the universities of Cambridge in England, Göttingen in Germany, Leiden in the Netherlands, and Zurich in Switzerland. At Cambridge he studied under Ernest Rutherford (1871-1937), the pioneer of subatomic physics. He obtained his Ph.D. at Göttingen where Werner Heisenberg (1901-1976) was studying quantum mechanics. In 1928 Oppenheimer became an assistant professor of physics at the University of California at Berkeley, where he developed theoretical physics (the study of matter and energy based on data rather than experimentation). He held a second post at the California Institute of Technology, Pasadena.

Oppenheimer's early work included the study of neutron stars—stars with a mass greater than that of the Sun that would eventually collapse to such a degree that their electrons and protons would be crushed together to make neutrons, or neutral elementary particles. Oppenheimer argued that such stars would collapse even further to become what would later be called "black holes," stars so dense that not even light escapes; but this view was only accepted in the 1960s.

NUCLEAR FISSION

In 1938 the German chemist Otto Hahn (1879-1968) was working with the element uranium. The heaviest of the natural elements, its atoms are unstable—short-lived or radioactive. In 1934 Italian physicist Enrico Fermi (1901-1954) found that when uranium is bombarded by subatomic particles called neutrons, several radioactive products are formed; he thought that they were radioactive isotopes similar to uranium 235. Hahn then found that one of the products of bombarded

KEY DATES

1904 April 22, born in New York

1925 Graduates from Harvard University, Cambridge, Massachusetts

1927 Receives doctorate from Göttingen University, Germany

1938 Nuclear fission is first observed

1942 The Manhattan Project to develop an atomic bomb is set up by the U.S. government

1943 Oppenheimer becomes director of the Manhattan Project laboratories based at Los Alamos, New Mexico

1945 July 16, first atom bomb successfully tested

1952 First hydrogen bomb tested

1953 Oppenheimer's security clearance is withdrawn

1955 Publishes *The Open Mind*, summarizing his philosophical ideas on science and society

1963 Is awarded the Atomic Energy Commission's highest honor, the Fermi Prize

1967 Dies in Princeton, New Jersey

Julius Robert Oppenheimer (left) is shown with Colonel Leslie Groves, who was in overall charge of the Manhattan Project to develop an atomic bomb. They are viewing the remains of the 100-foot (30-m) steel tower on which the world's first atomic bomb had been exploded two months earlier, in July 1945.

uranium was a radioactive form of the element barium. Hahn's colleague, Austrian physicist Lise Meitner (1878–1968), proposed that the production of barium was the result of the nucleus of the uranium atom being split in two to form two lighter nuclei. At the same time it emitted two or three neutrons, and released a large amount of energy.

Elements that can undergo fission are known as fissionable. Hahn and Meitner also found that the rarer U-235 isotope is more fissionable than the U-238 isotope that makes up 99.3 percent of natural uranium

(isotopes are atoms that have the same number of protons but a different number of neutrons in their nuclei). Once the reaction is set off in U-235, one neutron causes the release of three more neutrons (see diagram below left). Any of these new neutrons can now collide with another U-235 atom, so releasing another three neutrons, each of which can release three more neutrons, and so on, until there is no uranium left. This is called a chain reaction (see box opposite). Within less than a millionth of a second a chain reaction produces a massive release of energy.

Oppenheimer (far right) with Albert Einstein (1879–1955), who suggested the huge potential power of fusion and fission. In nuclear fission (below), a neutron bombards the nucleus of a uranium atom. The extra neutron causes the nucleus to split and release energy. Further neutrons are released to bombard further nuclei, causing a chain reaction.

Neutron

Nucleus of protons and neutrons

Heavy nucleus is split by the neutron

Neutrons released

Neutron released

DEVELOPING THE BOMB

World War II (1939–45) was about to break out, and scientists in Britain and the United States saw that nuclear fission could be used to create an extremely powerful bomb. Albert Einstein warned President Roosevelt (1882–1945) of the dangers of allowing Germany to develop such a weapon first. On December 6, 1941, a bomb project was set up under the direction of the Office of Scientific Research and Development.

By mid-1942 the War Department was brought into what became known as the "Manhattan Project," and Oppenheimer became its scientific director. Los Alamos, near Santa Fe, New Mexico, was chosen as the base for the laboratory, though the work employed thousands of workers in other locations.

The trust shown in Oppenheimer by his superiors was not shared by military security staff; the Federal Bureau of Investigation (FBI) advised against offering him the post on the Manhattan Project on the grounds that he was a communist sympathizer; his phone seems to have been tapped and his office bugged by FBI agents when he was working with the Manhattan Project. In August 1943, in an episode that has never been properly explained, Oppenheimer told military security agents that he had heard how secret information could be passed to Russia. He said Soviet agents had approached two of his colleagues, and he later implicated a friend. At security clearance hearings nearly a decade later Oppenheimer declared that what he had said in 1943 was "a tissue of lies."

THE FIRST CHAIN REACTION

The first controlled, self-sustaining chain reaction took place at the University of Chicago, Illinois, under the direction of the Italian-born U.S. physicist Enrico Fermi (1901–1954). A chain reaction is produced when an atomic nucleus is bombarded by neutrons to cause nuclear fission (see opposite).

In order to create the fission reaction, Fermi built a simple nuclear reactor. Rods of natural uranium were placed in a large pile of 40,000 graphite blocks known as "the pile." The purpose of the graphite was to slow down the fast neutrons emitted during fission so that they were more likely to cause further fissions than to escape from the pile. Rods made of cadmium absorbed stray neutrons and prevented a premature chain reaction from taking place.

The team who constructed the first atomic pile in 1942 are reunited at the University of Chicago (left). Enrico Fermi is in the front row, far left. The creation of the chain reaction is depicted in a painting (below), which clearly shows the enormous scale of the "pile."

On December 2, 1942, the cadmium control rods were removed. Counters set up to measure the rate of neutron production began to click; soon the clicks were so rapid that they became a continuous buzz, and Fermi confirmed that a chain reaction had started. Before a massive explosion occurred, the cadmium control rods were replaced and the reaction halted. The success of Fermi's dramatic experiment was relayed to other nuclear scientists in a coded message: "The Italian navigator has just landed in the New World."

"Little Boy" (above), the atomic fission bomb that was dropped on Hiroshima weighed just 4.5 tons (4 tonnes), but it flattened 4 square miles (6 sq km) of the city. One of the few buildings not annihilated by the blast was the Museum of Science and Industry (left).

illustrated by two early fatalities at Los Alamos, caused by accidents when handling the radioactive material.

THE SHATTERER OF WORLDS

The first atomic bomb, "Fat Man," was tested on July 16, 1945 in the New Mexico desert. Many of the project scientists watched the explosion from just 5 miles (8 km) away—no one then knew of the risks of radiation fallout. Oppenheimer recalled the event: "There floated through my mind a line from the Bhagavad-Gita [an epic Indian poem]: "I am become death, the shatterer of worlds." The explosion lit up the sky, and it was estimated that the bomb generated a power equivalent to about 20,000 tons of TNT explosive.

On August 6, 1945 an atomic bomb using U-235 was dropped on Hiroshima, Japan, killing 80,000 civilians. Three days later a second atomic bomb using plutonium was dropped on Nagasaki. About 40,000 people were killed outright. On August 15 Japan surrendered unconditionally, bringing World War II to an end. Within a year another 150,000 victims had died as a result of the explosions and, for decades after, thousands more died of radiation sickness and suffered other health problems. Oppenheimer resigned from the Manhattan Project in October 1945.

Meanwhile, scientists faced problems on the Manhattan Project. The first difficulty was how to produce enough fissionable U-235. To produce just a small amount of fissionable U-235 required vast amounts of electricity and much complicated machinery. Eventually another fissionable isotope—plutonium 239—was employed, but even this needed massive chemical reactors to be built.

A chain reaction will cause an explosion only if there is a certain minimum amount of fissionable material; this is called the "critical mass." The problem was to assemble a critical mass without it exploding on its own. The dangers of this work were tragically

AN EVEN MORE DEADLY BOMB

Edward Teller (see box below) had argued in favor of developing a hydrogen bomb (H-bomb). This involves a process called nuclear fusion (see diagram right). On August 29, 1949 the Soviet Union announced that it had exploded its first fission bomb. Teller repeated his call for a "superbomb."

Oppenheimer was by now chairman of the General Advisory Committee of the Atomic Energy Commission. In 1949 it stated its opposition to development of the hydrogen bomb, concluding that there was "no limit to its explosive power." However, President Harry S. Truman (1884–1972) was persuaded that there was no alternative but to develop the H-bomb—the need to beat the Soviet Union in this new arms race had become of paramount importance. On November 1, 1952 the first hydrogen bomb was exploded by the United States at Eniwetok Atoll, Marshall Islands, in the Pacific Ocean. The bomb's explosive power was 500 times more than the bomb dropped on Nagasaki.

ACCUSATIONS AND CHARGES

On August 12, 1953 the Soviet Union claimed to have exploded a hydrogen bomb. The shock of finding that the Soviet Union was pulling ahead in the weapons race heightened the antagonism toward communism. Questions were asked about why the Atomic Energy Commission and Oppenheimer, its chief scientist, had been slow to support the development of the H-bomb. On December 21, 1953 charges were leveled against Oppenheimer: that he had mixed with communists; that he had recruited communists to Los Alamos; that he had tried to delay work on the superbomb; and that he was probably a Soviet spy. His security clearance, which allowed him access to secret information, was removed.

To clear his name, Oppenheimer went before a security hearing. He was declared not guilty of treason, but his security clearance was not returned and his post as advisor to the Atomic Energy Commission was terminated. One of those who testified against Oppenheimer was Teller. He insisted that Oppenheimer was "loyal to the United States," but he added that he would "prefer to see the vital interests of

In nuclear fusion the atoms of two light elements are joined to form a heavier element. Heavy isotopes of hydrogen— tritium and deuterium—are fused to create a helium nucleus, releasing a neutron and massive amounts of energy.

Helium

Energy

Neutron

Deuterium

Tritium

this country in hands that I understand better and therefore trust more." Oppenheimer's reputation was restored in 1963 when, as an apology for the treatment he had received, he was awarded the Atomic Energy Commission's highest honor, the Fermi Prize, which he collected from President Lyndon B. Johnson (1908–1973). He died four years later of throat cancer.

Edward Teller
1908–2003

Theoretical physicist Dr. Edward Teller, often called the "father of the H-bomb," joined Fermi's team working on the first chain reaction experiment at the University of Chicago in 1942. He also worked on the Manhattan Project at Los Alamos. In 1952 he headed a nuclear weapons research facility, the Lawrence Livermore Laboratory at Berkeley, California. Teller testified against Oppenheimer in 1954 and lobbied to keep the United States ahead in the nuclear arms race during the Cold War. In the 1980s Teller became the driving force behind the Strategic Defense Initiative championed by President Ronald Reagan (1911–2004).

JULIUS ROBERT OPPENHEIMER

SCIENTIFIC BACKGROUND

Before 1930

The French physicists Antoine Becquerel (1852-1908), Marie Curie (1867-1934), and Pierre Curie (1859-1906) pioneer the study of atomic radiation

The New Zealand-born British physicist Ernest Rutherford (1871-1937) and the Danish physicist Niels Bohr (1885-1962) develop models of the atom in which a nucleus of protons (positively charged particles) is orbited by electrons (negatively charged particles)

The German-born physicist Albert Einstein (1879-1955) predicts that matter can be converted into energy

1932 The positron (antielectron), a particle that is exactly like an electron but behaves as if it has a positive charge, is discovered; the existence of such antiparticles was predicted in 1928 by English physicist Paul Dirac (1902-1984)

1932 English physicist James Chadwick (1891-1974) discovers a neutral atomic particle, the neutron

1934 Italian physicist Enrico Fermi (1901-1954) discovers that when uranium is bombarded with neutrons, several radioactive products are formed

1938 German physicist Otto Hahn (1879-1968) finds that a radioactive form of the much lighter element barium is produced when the uranium atom is bombarded

1939 Otto Hahn's student Lise Meitner (1878-1968) confirms that Hahn has "split" the uranium atom, and calculates that large amounts of energy can be produced by this process, called nuclear fission

1940 In Birmingham, England, two German refugee physicists, Otto Frisch (1904-1979) and Rudolf Peierls (1907-1995), establish that only a few pounds of uranium-235 would be necessary to make an atomic chain reaction possible

1942 At the University of Chicago, the first controlled, self-sustaining nuclear chain reaction is achieved by Enrico Fermi

1943 The main laboratories of the Manhattan Project, the Allied project to develop an atomic bomb, are set up at Los Alamos, New Mexico; Oppenheimer is scientific director

1930   1935   1940

POLITICAL AND CULTURAL BACKGROUND

1932 At the Olympic Games in Los Angeles 18-year-old American typist Mildred "Babe" Didrikson (1914-1956) wins gold medals in the javelin and the 80-meter hurdles and a silver medal in the high jump

1933 In Germany a crackdown on any area of the arts that does not conform to Nazi theory leads to the burning of books that are "un-German" or by Jewish authors, and the closure of the influential Bauhaus school of design

1936 Civil war breaks out in Spain as General Francisco Franco (1892-1975) sets up a rival government. He will rule the entire country from 1939

1938 The House UnAmerican Activities Committee, set up to investigate political extremism by the House of Representatives, focuses almost exclusively on the perceived "communist infiltration" of American society

1941 Japanese bombers attack the American Pacific fleet at anchor in Pearl Harbor, Hawaii, prompting the United States to enter World War II (1939-45)

1943 In the largest tank battle in history, at Kursk, south of Moscow, the Soviet Red Army inflicts a massive defeat on the Germans

1944 Japanese pilots begin launching kamikaze ("divine wind") suicide missions on Allied ships; in 1,465 Japanese attacks more than 3,000 Allied sailors are killed

1945 The first atomic bomb is tested at Trinity, New Mexico

1945 On August 6 and 9, United States airplanes drop atomic bombs on the cities of Hiroshima and Nagasaki in Japan; Japan surrenders, bringing World War II (1939–45) to an end

1949 The General Advisory Committee to the Atomic Energy Commission, of which Oppenheimer is chairman, advises against development of the hydrogen bomb

1949 The Soviet Union tests its first atomic bomb

1951 The Hungarian-born physicist Edward Teller (1908–2003) becomes scientific director of the project to build a hydrogen bomb at Los Alamos

1952 In a test at Eniwetok Atoll in the Pacific, the first American hydrogen bomb explodes with 500 times the force of the atomic bomb that fell on Nagasaki

1953 The Soviet Union tests its first hydrogen bomb

1958 An experimental nuclear reactor for generating electricity opens at Shippingport, Pennsylvania

1963 Oppenheimer receives the Enrico Fermi Prize, the highest honor of the U.S. Atomic Energy Commission

1967 China detonates its first hydrogen bomb

After 1970

1985 Edward Teller convinces President Ronald Reagan (1911–2004) to seek billions of dollars from Congress in order to develop the Strategic Defense Initiative ("Star Wars"), to consist of powerful lasers in orbit, that are capable of shooting down enemy intercontinental ballistic missiles; a similar plan is resurrected by President George W. Bush (1946–) in 2001

(1945)   (1950)   (1955)   (1960)   (1965)

1949 *South Pacific*, a stage musical by Richard Rodgers (1902–1979) and Oscar Hammerstein II (1895–1960), enjoys a huge success on Broadway in New York and wins the Pulitzer Prize

1950 Senator Joseph McCarthy (1908–1957) claims to have proof that 205 officials in the State Department are communists; although he fails to prove a case against anyone, the careers of hundreds of innocent people are ruined

1955 The original Disneyland opens in Anaheim, California

1955 South Africa withdraws from the United Nations General Assembly after the U.N. refuses to uphold South Africa's racist "apartheid" policies; this marks the beginning of the country's long period of political isolation

1957 English novelist Ian Fleming (1908–1964) publishes *From Russia with Love*, one of 12 novels featuring secret service agent James Bond, known as 007

1960 Soviet airforce major Yuri Gagarin (1934–1968) completes an orbit of the earth in *Vostok I*, the world's first manned spaceship

1963 Martin Luther King Jr. (1929–1968) leads more than 200,000 people in a march on Washington to demand civil rights for black Americans

1964 The Beatles release their pop singles "She Loves You" and "I Want to Hold Your Hand" in the United States, and trigger a wave of "Beatlemania" when they tour the country for the first time

RICHARD FEYNMAN

1918–1988

"If it disagrees with experiment it is wrong. In that simple statement is the key to science. It does not make any difference how beautiful your guess is. It does not make any difference how smart you are...if it disagrees with experiment it is wrong."

Richard Feynman
Messenger Lectures, Cornell University (1964)

ONE OF THE GREATEST OF ALL THEORETICAL PHYSICISTS, RICHARD FEYNMAN HELPED TO MAKE SCIENCE MORE EASILY UNDERSTOOD THROUGH HIS LECTURES AND BOOKS. HE HELPED FORMULATE THE THEORY OF QUANTUM ELECTRODYNAMICS, FOR WHICH HE SHARED THE 1965 NOBEL PRIZE FOR PHYSICS, AND HE ALSO STUDIED "SUPERFLUIDITY" IN LIQUID HELIUM AND THE "WEAK" AND "STRONG" INTERACTIONS BETWEEN PARTICLES.

Born on May 11, 1918, in New York City to a Byelorussian immigrant father and a mother who was the daughter of a Polish immigrant, Feynman had an imaginative mind and was a gifted mathematician able to solve complex problems. He was fascinated by physics, too, and intrigued by the quantum theory developed in the 1920s. He graduated from the Massachusetts Institute of Technology (MIT) in 1939, and in that year he moved to Princeton University in New Jersey to carry out postgraduate research.

SUCCESS AT LOS ALAMOS

In 1941 the United States entered World War II (1939–45), and Feynman joined the Manhattan Project to help develop the atomic bomb. At first he worked from MIT, but later moved to Los Alamos, New Mexico, where the Project was based. At Los Alamos, Feynman's talents were quickly recognized, and he was made head of the theoretical computation group. In those days there were no computers, and the group had to carry out hugely complicated calculations to predict how neutrons might behave in atomic explosions.

Success in his work was marred by personal tragedy when his first wife died of tuberculosis in July 1945, a few months before scientists from Los Alamos exploded the world's first atomic bomb.

After the Manhattan Project ended, Feynman went to Cornell University, New York, where he joined the physics department run by German-born American physicist Hans Bethe (1906–2005), who had been the director of theoretical physics at Los Alamos. Feynman began investigating how forces such as light, electricity, and magnetism work together. This led to his interest in quantum electrodynamics.

FRENKEL FIELDS

$$\int K(x,x')\Psi(x',t)dx'$$

$$= A e^{\frac{i\epsilon}{\hbar} L\left(\frac{x-x'}{\epsilon}, x\right)}$$

$$t^2 - R^2 \cong a^2$$

$$t = \sqrt{R^2 + a^2}$$

$$\approx R + \frac{a^2}{2R}$$

KEY DATES

1939 Graduates from Massachusetts Institute of Technology

1942 Gains doctorate from Princeton University, N.J.

1942–45 Works at Los Alamos on the atomic bomb

1959 Nanotechnology first described

1963 Publishes *The Feynman Lectures on Physics*

1965 Shares the Nobel Prize for physics with Julian Schwinger and Sin-Itiro Tomonaga

1985 *Surely You're Joking, Mr. Feynman!* published

1986 Appointed member of the Rogers Commission on the *Challenger* disaster

1988 Publishes *What Do You Care What Other People Think?*

Richard Feynman lecturing at the European Organization for Nuclear Research (CERN) near Geneva, Switzerland. Although a great physicist, he was also an extraordinary communicator.

WHAT IS QUANTUM ELECTRODYNAMICS?

Quantum theory deals with interactions between small-scale particles such as electrons, including the small-scale interactions in light and other types of radiation. Electromagnetism deals with the interaction between electrical and magnetic fields, and also describes light. Quantum electrodynamics (QED) is the quantum theory of electromagnetism: it describes the electromagnetic force between subatomic particles in terms of the exchange of photons—the "particles" of light described by Albert Einstein (1879–1955) in 1905. In the normal world, QED explains everything that gravity does not.

Quantum electrodynamics began with the work of British theoretical physicist Paul Dirac (1902–1984). In 1928 physicists were aware of only two types of nuclear particles: the negatively charged electron and the positively charged proton. In that year, however, Dirac published an equation that seemed to predict a particle that was exactly like an electron, but which had a positive charge. This is an example of an "antiparticle." Four years later Dirac's theory was confirmed when the positron (antielectron) was discovered. Dirac's work was developed from 1945 by American physicist Julian Schwinger (1918–1994), working at Harvard University.

STARTING AGAIN

Feynman refused to rely on work done previously by other physicists, and was therefore forced "to rediscover or reinvent for himself almost the whole of physics." He needed to be able to picture the movements of atoms or electrons as they interacted.

In Feynman's method for calculating the interaction between electrons, positrons, and photons, he used diagrams to show how particles moved from one space–time point to another. If light is transmitted from A to B, it could be assumed that the photons of light follow a single direct path connecting A and B by the shortest route. Experiments indicated, however, that quantum particles did not always move in this way.

A beryllium atom model (above) shows electrons orbiting the nucleus. Scientists know there are many smaller particles that move in a complex way: the image (right) shows the destruction of an antiproton (line entering left) and a proton at the intersection point right of center. The spiral tracks are caused by low-energy electrons and positrons.

Murray Gell-Mann
1929–

Murray Gell-Mann is an American theoretical physicist. In 1956 he was appointed professor of physics (and, in 1967, of theoretical physics) at the California Institute of Technology (CalTech).

In the 20th century the atom model had become complex. In 1953 Gell-Mann proposed reclassifying particles such as the neutron and proton with a new quantum number—the "strangeness number"—in order to explain their behavior. In 1964 he suggested a further level of complexity in the atom model by arguing that protons were not fundamental particles, but were made up of "quarks," subatomic particles that have fractional charges ($+^2/_3$ or $^1/_3$, for example), and occur in twos or threes. It is thought that there are three quarks inside each proton and three inside each neutron. Gell-Mann was awarded the Nobel Prize for physics in 1969.

Feynman suggested that the photons take every path connecting A and B. Some swerve a little before reaching B, others travel vast distances, veering off in different directions before returning to B. Feynman argued that an infinite number of paths needs to be considered in order to determine the most probable route of the photon. Using what are now known as Feynman diagrams, Feynman showed how the probabilities for all these paths could be added up to provide an answer that agreed with known experiments.

Meanwhile Japanese physicist Sin-Itiro Tomonaga (1906–1979) had compiled a version of QED by 1943. However, his research was published in 1947, by which time Schwinger and Feynman had produced their results. Tomonaga, Schwinger, and Feynman received the 1965 Nobel Prize for physics for work in this area.

STRANGE HAPPENINGS

Temperature can be defined in terms of particle movement. The more violent the motion, the higher the temperature. At the other end of the scale is the

temperature at which each particle has the minimum amount of motion according to the uncertainty principle. The uncertainty principle states that we cannot know both the position and the momentum of a particle at the same time. This means that a particle cannot possess zero energy (be stationary) because then we would know both its position and momentum. The point at which a particle has the minimum amount of motion possible is called absolute zero, or zero Kelvin (K), equivalent to $-273.16°C$.

If elements are cooled to very low temperatures they may display some strange properties. In 1911 Dutch physicist Heike Kamerlingh Onnes (1853–1926) reported that when mercury was cooled to about 4K, its electrical resistance disappeared. This meant that an electric current passed through mercury at this temperature would run forever because of the lack of resistance, or "drag," in the mercury. Onnes also managed to lower the temperature of helium to 0.8K, at which its electrical resistance also decreased. This phenomenon was later named "superconductivity."

The Russian physicist Pyotr Kapitza (1894–1984) then experimented with a substance called helium II. This exists below a temperature of 2.2K. In 1938 he reported that helium II flows so freely that once set spinning in a container it will flow without stopping. This property is known as superfluidity. Between 1953 and 1958 Feynman used quantum mechanics to explain the superfluidity of helium II.

Superconductivity was eventually explained by Nobel prizewinning American physicists John Bardeen (1908–1991), Leon Cooper (1930–), and John Robert Schrieffer (1931–). They showed that in certain

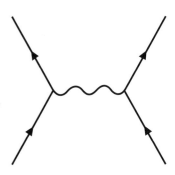

A Feynman diagram with two electrons approaching each other and exchanging a force-carrying particle (here, a photon). The wiggly line represents all possible ways in which the photon could have moved.

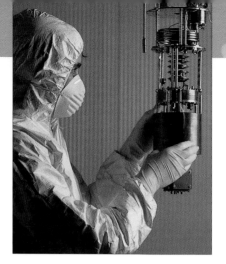

circumstances, usually low temperatures, drifting electrons link in pairs known as Cooper pairs and resistance to their movement is removed, so the flow of electrons can continue indefinitely through the superconducting material.

The four key forces in nature are gravity, electromagnetism, and—at the atomic level—forces known as the "weak" and "strong" interactions. In 1958 Feynman and Gell-Mann produced a paper on the weak interaction theory, a complex equation describing beta decay, a type of radiation released by certain atoms as they break down. Feynman was still little known outside his field, but that changed when he made the unprecedented decision to teach freshman physics at the California Institute of Technology (Caltech), near Los Angeles, where he had been professor since 1950.

At the Gran Sasso Laboratory in Italy, a scientist investigates the type of radiation known as beta decay. Feynman's final major contribution to physics was the weak interaction theory, developed with Gell-Mann, which described the beta decay of neutrons.

The talks, delivered from 1961 to 1963, were transcribed and published as *The Feynman Lectures in Physics.* Feynman's lively and accessible approach to the subject had an enormous impact on physicists around the world.

In the last decade of his life Richard Feynman became more widely known, mainly due to his work on the *Challenger* commission and the great success of his two autobiographical works, *Surely You're Joking, Mr. Feynman!* (1985) and *What Do You Care What Other People Think?* (1988).

SMALL WORLD

Miniaturization is now a familiar part of our world, but Feynman was one of the first scientists to take seriously the possibility of "nanotechnology": engineering on a tiny scale. In 1959 he gave a talk at the annual meeting of the American Physical Society at CalTech entitled, "There is Plenty of Room at the Bottom." He chose this title because he wanted to stress that the laws of physics allowed many ways in which engineering could take place on the scale of atoms and molecules. He suggested, for example, that if letters were represented by a code of dots and dashes, and if each "bit" of information were stored on a cube of metal made up of about 125 atoms, then 24 million books could be stored on a cube of material $1/200$-inch wide. By 1995 scientists at the Los Alamos National Laboratory were storing readable text on steel pins measuring 2.5 x 0.2 cm; each carried two gigabytes, the equivalent of about 1,000 standard books.

At the lecture Feynman announced his intention of offering $1,000 to the first person to build a working

MIT graduate student Brian Hubert with his Nano Assembly Machine. It is able to pick up and assemble virtually any type of material, several thousand atoms at a time. The Nano Assembly Machine won Hubert the MIT-Lemelson Student Prize for Inventiveness in 2001.

electric motor that would fit within a $1/64$-inch cube. The prize was won the following year. Feynman also challenged someone to take information from the page of a book and put it on an area $1/25,000$ of the original page size so that it could be read by an electron microscope. In 1985 Tom Newman, a graduate student at Stanford University, claimed the prize.

RICHARD FEYNMAN

SCIENTIFIC BACKGROUND

Before 1940

Dutch physicist Heike Onnes (1853-1926) discovers superconductivity

Anti-particles are explained by French physicist Louis-Victor de Broglie (1892-1987)

Russian physicist Pyotr Kapitza (1894-1984) describes superfluidity

1942 Feynman works at Los Alamos on the Manhattan Project, designing the first atomic bomb

1943 Japanese scientist Sin-Itiro Tomonaga (1906-1979) compiles a version of QED

1948 American physicist Julian Schwinger (1918-1994) presents his version of QED

1949 Feynman develops another approach to QED using his "method of path integrals" or "sum over histories"

1953-58 In a series of papers, Feynman uses quantum mechanics to explain the superfluidity of helium II

1955 A new model of liquid helium is proposed

1958 In collaboration with the American physicist Murray Gell-Mann (1929-) Feynman publishes a paper on the weak interaction theory, a complex equation describing beta decay

1959 Feynman delivers a lecture on nanotechnology, engineering on a tiny scale

1963 *The Feynman Lectures on Physics* are published

1964 American physicist Peter Higgs (1929-) proposes the existence of the still undetected Higgs particle

1965 Feynman shares the Nobel Prize for Physics with Sin-Itiro Tomonaga and Julian Schwinger for their work on QED

1970s Feynman and researcher Richard Field investigate quark jets using quantum chromodynamics (QCD), a theory of the interaction between quarks

1972 American physicists John Bardeen (1908-1991), Leon Cooper (1930-), and John Robert Schrieffer (1931-) win the Nobel Prize for physics for their work on superconductivity

After 1980

1984 Superstring theory unites quantum mechanics, particle physics, and gravity

1986 Feynman serves on the *Challenger* commission enquiry

1988 Feynman publishes *What Do You Care What Other People Think?*

1940   **1950**   **1960**   **1970**

POLITICAL AND CULTURAL BACKGROUND

1944 Fifteen-year-old Anne Frank (1929-1945) and her Jewish family are discovered by the Nazis in Amsterdam, Netherlands, and sent to concentration camps

1946 In the aftermath of World War II (1939-45), the Allies stage major war crimes trials in Japan and Nuremberg, Germany

1947 *A Streetcar Named Desire*, by American playwright Tennessee Williams (1911-1983), wins the Pulitzer Prize; Williams will win the prize again for *Cat on a Hot Tin Roof* (1955)

1955 The Japanese company Sony launches its first mass-produced transistor radio

1955 Argentinian president Juan Domingo Péron (1895-1974) is deposed by the army and flees to Spain

1960 In Sharpeville, South Africa, police open fire on a demonstration by black citizens; 69 people are killed

1964 In the United States the Civil Rights Act is passed, banning discrimination on the grounds of race, color, religion, or sex

1967 *The Graduate* features rising star Dustin Hoffman (1937-); its director, Mike Nichols (1931-) wins an Academy Award for the film

1970 Soviet author Aleksandr Solzhenitsyn (1918-) is awarded the Nobel Prize for literature for his novels *Cancer Ward* and *The First Circle*, both of which have been banned in the Soviet Union

1974 India tests its first nuclear bomb

1976 An army coup in Argentina deposes the president Isabelita Perón (1931-), the second wife of Juan Perón. Military rule will last until 1983

GLOSSARY

Absolute zero (zero Kelvin) The lowest theoretical temperature; measured in Kelvin, the equivalent to -273.16°C.

Acceleration The rate of change in velocity of a moving body due to force acting on it.

Anode A positively charged electrode.

Astronomy The study of the origin, motion, and composition of material in the universe.

Astrophysics The study of the nature of celestial bodies and events.

Atom One of the tiny, indivisible particles of which material objects are composed, and since the 20th century the name given to the package of matter made up of at least two subatomic particles.

Atomic bomb A highly destructive weapon that depends on nuclear fission.

Atomic nucleus The positively charged dense region at the center of an atom.

Atomic number The number of protons in an atomic nucleus.

Black hole The possible final state of a star, when its mass and gravitational pull become so great that it collapses inward to become an object of zero size and infinite density.

Cathode A negatively charged electrode.

Chain reaction A reaction that is self-sustaining; each step triggers the next.

Chemical bonds The forces of attraction that hold together atoms to form molecules.

Electric current A flow of electric charge through a conductor.

Electricity The effect of charged particles at rest and in motion. Electricity is used to provide a very adaptable form of energy.

Electrode Any terminal by which an electric current passes in or out of a substance able to conduct electricity.

Electromagnetic force The interaction between bodies carrying electric charge.

Electromagnetic radiation The form in which energy is transmitted through space or matter.

Electromagnetism The study of electric and magnetic fields, and their interaction with electric charges and electric currents.

Electron A negatively charged subatomic particle orbiting the nucleus of an atom.

Element Any substance that cannot be split chemically into simpler substances.

Energy The capacity to do work.

Gamma rays High-energy photons.

Gravity The force of attraction between all matter.

Helium A gas, lighter than all the other elements except hydrogen.

Hydrogen The simplest, lightest element; a colorless gas. It is believed that all other elements were produced by hydrogen fusion.

Ion An atom or group of atoms that has become electrically charged.

Isotope Atoms of a chemical element that have the same number of protons in the nucleus, but different numbers of neutrons.

Light Electromagnetic radiation to which the human eye is sensitive.

Light-year A unit of distance equal to the distance traveled by light in a vacuum in one sidereal year (a year measured in respect of fixed stars)—equal to about 5.88 trillion miles.

Magnetism The phenomenon associated with magnetic dipoles. A permanent magnet has two poles, one of which always seeks the north (the north pole), and one of which always seeks the south (the south pole).

Mass A measure of the extent to which an object resists acceleration when a force is applied to it; also, a measure of the amount of matter in an object.

Matter That which occupies space and has mass; solids, liquids, and gases.

Motion Movement; the process of change in the position of one object relative to another.

Neutron One of the three main subatomic particles, along with electrons and protons.

Nuclear energy Energy released from an atomic nucleus during a nuclear reaction.

Nuclear fission The splitting of the nucleus of a heavy atom into two lighter nuclei.

Nuclear fusion A nuclear reaction in which the nuclei of light atoms combine to produce heavier nuclei, releasing vast energy.

Nuclear reaction A process in which the structure and energy content of an atomic nucleus is changed by interreaction with another nucleus or particle.

Periodic table A table in which the elements are arranged in order of their atomic number.

Physics The science dealing with the properties of matter and energy.

Proton A positively charged subatomic particle in the atomic nucleus.

Quantum mechanics Fundamental theory, developed in the early 20th century, of small-scale physical phenomena, such as the motions of electrons and nuclei within atoms.

Radiation The emission and transfer through space of electromagnetic radiation or subatomic particles.

Radioactivity The spontaneous disintegration of certain unstable nuclei, accompanied by the emission of alpha particles, beta rays, or gamma rays.

Radiograph A photograph exposed with X-rays or gamma rays.

Radioisotope A radioactive isotope of an element.

Reaction, chemical A process that involves changes in the structure and energy content of atoms, molecules, or ions.

Relativity, theory of A theory developed by Albert Einstein regarding the nature of space, time, and matter.

Spectrum, electromagnetic The range of electromagnetic radiations arranged according to their wavelengths, of which a part is the visible spectrum.

Subatomic particle Any particle that is smaller than an atom.

Superconductivity A condition occurring for example in many metals at low temperatures, in which electrical resistance (opposition to flow of electricity) disappears.

Theoretical physics The branch of physics in which theories of matter and energy are based on logical reasoning using known information.

X-ray Any of the highly energetic rays situated next to gamma rays on the electromagnetic spectrum.

FURTHER RESOURCES

PUBLICATIONS
ASTRONOMY
Anderson, Margaret J. *Isaac Newton: The Greatest Scientist of All Time.* Springfield, NJ: Enslow, 2008.

Hoskin, Michael, ed. *The Cambridge Concise History of Astronomy.* New York: Cambridge University Press, 1999.

Silverberg, Robert. *Four Men Who Changed the Universe.* New York: Putnam, 1968.

CHEMISTRY
Greenberg, Arthur. *A Chemical History Tour: Picturing Chemistry from Alchemy to Modern Molecular Science.* New York: Wiley, 2000.

Hirshfeld, Alan W. *The Electric Life of Michael Faraday.* New York: Walkerbooks,2006.

Stwertka, Albert. *A Guide to the Elements.* Rev. ed. New York: Oxford University Press, 2002.

Time-Life Books. *Structure of Matter.* Alexandria, VA: Time-Life, 1992.

COSMOLOGY
Hawley, John F., and Katherine A. Holcombe. *Foundations of Modern Cosmology.* New York: Oxford University Press, 2005.

Kallen, Stuart A. *Exploring the Origins of the Universe.* New York: Twenty-First Century Books, 1997.

Rasmussen, Richard Michael. *Mysteries of Space: Opposing Viewpoints.* San Diego, CA: Greenhaven, 1994.

Stannard, Russell. *Our Universe: A Guide to What's Out There.* New York: Kingfisher, 1995.

Swisher, Clarice. *Relativity: Opposing Viewpoints.* San Diego, CA: Greenhaven, 1990.

Trefil, James S. *The Moment of Creation: Big Bang Physics from Before the First Millisecond to the Present Universe.* Mineola, NY: Dover, 2004.

Weinberg, Steven. *Cosmology.* New York: Oxford University Press, 2008.

PHYSICS
Asimov, Isaac. *The History of Physics.* New York: Walker, 1984.

Barrow, John D. *Theories of Everything: The Quest for Ultimate Explanation.* New York: Oxford University Press, 1991.

Bernstein, Jeremy. *Albert Einstein and the Frontiers of Physics.* New York: Oxford University Press, 1997.

Blin-Stoyle, Roger J. *Eureka! Physics of Particles, Matter, and the Universe.* Philadelphia, PA: Institute of Physics, 1997.

Bloomfield, Louis. *How Things Work: The Physics of Everyday Life.* 4th ed. New York: Wiley, 2009.

Feynman, Richard P. *Six Easy Pieces: Essentials of Physics, Explained by Its Most Brilliant Teacher.* New York: Basic Books, 2005.

Fleisher, Paul. *Secrets of the Universe: Discovering the Universal Laws of Science.* New York: Atheneum, 1987.

Gindikin, Semen Grigorevich. *Tales of Physicists and Mathematicians.* Trans. Alan Shuchat. Boston: Birkhauser, 1988.

Goldberg, Jake. *Albert Einstein.* Danbury, CN.: Franklin Watts, 1996.

Grady, Sean M. *Marie Curie.* San Diego, Calif.: Lucent, 1992.

Gribbin, John, and Mary Gribbin. *Richard Feynman: A Life in Science.* New York: Viking, 1997.

Jespersen, James. *Looking at the Invisible Universe.* New York: Atheneum, 1990.

Jewett, John W. *The World of Physics: Mysteries, Magic and Myth.* Fort Worth, TX: Harcourt College, 2001.

Leighton, Ralph, and Richard Feynman. *"Surely You're Joking, Mr. Feynman!": Adventures of a Curious Character.* New York: Vintage, 2007.

Lerner, Aaron Bunsen. *Einstein and Newton: A Comparison of the Two Greatest Scientists.* Minneapolis: Lerner, 1973.

McClaffery, Carla Killough. *"Something Out of Nothing: Marie Curie and Radium.* New York: Farrar, Straus and Giroux 2006.

Meadows, A. J., and M. M. Hancock-Beaulieu. *Front Page Physics: A Century of Physics in the News.* Philadelphia, PA: Institute of Physics, 1994.

Pasachoff, Naomi E. *Marie Curie and the Science of Radioactivity.* New York: Oxford University Press, 1997.

Paul, Richard. *A Handbook to the Universe: Explorations of Matter, Energy, Space, and Time for Beginning Scientific Thinkers.* Chicago: Chicago Review Press, 1993.

Russell, Colin A. *Michael Faraday: Physics and Faith.* New York: Oxford University Press, 2001.

Shamos, Morris H., ed. *Great Experiments in Physics: Firsthand Accounts from Galileo to Einstein.* New York: Dover, 1987.

Spangenburg, Ray, and Diane Kit Moser. *Niels Bohr: Atomic Theorist.* New York: Chelsea House, 2008.

Stwertka, Albert, and Eve Stwertka. *Physics: From Newton to the Big Bang.* New York: Franklin Watts, 1986.

WEBSITES
GENERAL SCIENCE
The Exploratorium
www.exploratorium.edu
A museum of science, art, and human perception located in San Francisco, California. Included in the site are more than 10,000 web pages and hundreds of sound and video files, exploring hundreds of different topics. Includes a variety of online exhibits that allow visitors to interact with the activity, instructions for more than 200 simple experiments, webcast interviews, tours, and learning tools.

ASTRONOMY
National Radio Astronomy Observatory
www.nrao.edu
A research facility of the U.S. National Science Foundation that designs, builds, operates, and maintains radio telescopes used by scientists from around the world. Website provides an introduction to radio astronomy, along with an image gallery, general astronomy information, information about specific radio telescopes, and more.

COSMOLOGY
Introduction to Cosmology
http://map.gsfc.nasa.gov/html/web_site.html
Part of the Microwave Anisotropy Probe (MAP) website at NASA. Introduces basic concepts in modern cosmology and describes the MAP mission, which probes conditions in the early universe.

PHYSICS
The Laws List
www.alcyone.com/max/physics/laws/index.html
List of various laws, rules, principles, and other related topics in physics and astronomy.
Physics 2000
www.colorado.edu/physics/2000/index.pl
Interactive exploration of the field of physics, including explanations of how the study of physics has made possible various pieces of common technology.
PhysicsWeb
http://physicsworld.com/cws/home
Current news in physics, book reviews, and a digest of notable recent articles in the field.

INDEX